Mary T. .ney

The Road to the Gallows

For my mother

Mary Timney

The Road to the Gallows

Mary Timney

Jayne Baldwin

Published by
Clayhole Publishing
15 Lochryan Street
Stranraer
DG9 7HP

ISBN 978 0 9569331 1 9

Printed by
J & B Print
32a Albert Street
Newton Stewart
DG8 6EJ

layout and design by Mike Clayton
mj.clayton@btinternet.com

Front cover image: original pen and ink sketch by Shalla Gray
Back cover: copy of Mary's signature, courtesy of National Records of Scotland

Contents

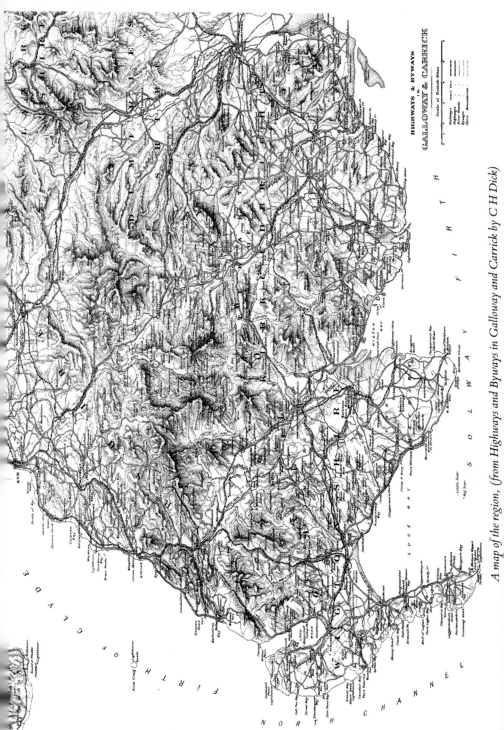

A map of the region, (from Highways and Byways in Galloway and Carrick by C H Dick)

"A murderess is only an ordinary woman in a temper."
Edith Bagnold

A thrill of horror ran through the court room as the judge, dubbed Lord Death, donned the black cap and began to address the slight young woman sitting in the dock. After an exhausting day of evidence the jury had taken only twenty minutes to decide she was guilty of brutally bludgeoning her neighbour to death. Mary Timney, wearing her best hat, a small green trimmed straw bonnet with its shabby gum flowers, had watched witness after witness condemn her; her neighbours, people she'd grown up with in the remote Scottish glen. Worst of all, she'd seen her own young daughters brought into court to be bullied into giving evidence against her. She'd sat impassively through the long hours of her trial for murder in a shocked, uncomprehending silence. But at the sight of the black cap on the judge's bewigged head Mary finally understood the gravity of her situation and broke down pleading for her life. Begging to be spared from the humiliation of a public hanging Mary sobbed and cried; the people in the packed public gallery were moved despite the horrifying details of the case and her attempts to implicate her own mother. For weeks Mary had been portrayed in the newspapers as a "savage and implacable monster" but the sight of her in distress, prompted sympathy even from those who had just pronounced her guilty. The judge remained unmoved. Stony faced Lord Deas intoned: "The time of all of us in this world is short, with most of us it is uncertain, but it is necessarily short in your case. Your days are numbered. They must indeed, be very few."

One

"The spot where the bloody deed occurred wears a solitary and unfrequented appearance."

Agnes McLellan trudged, reluctantly, along the turnpike road towards Carsphad, there was snow on the hills and the cold winter wind snatched at her woollen shawl. It wasn't just that she didn't want to venture out on this bleak Monday in January; she had no wish to go to the cottage of Mary Reid, or Timney as she'd been called since her marriage. The two women had known each other for many years, both growing up in the huddle of small cottages near the Polharrow bridge, though Agnes, known as Nan to everyone in this small community, was almost ten years older than Mary. Nan had no time for her and neither did her friend Ann Hannah, Mary's nearest neighbour; the two of them had often discussed the younger woman's many flaws, her poor housekeeping, ill temper and drinking among them. As Nan walked the half mile from her father's home where she still kept house, she grumbled about Mary's gall at sending her eldest girl to ask her to come to the cottage to bake. It had been noon when Susan Timney had chapped at the door to say that her mother was in bed poorly; Nan had told the girl she would go up after she'd had her bit o' dinner.

The turnpike road steadily climbed past New Galloway in the south of the Glenkens through St John's Town of Dalry, known to locals as the Clachan, and on to Carsphairn on the border with Ayrshire. Although there was a daily coach taking passengers from Castle Douglas north to Ayr, there was little else in the way of traffic in the first days of 1862.

2

Although the farmhouse at Carsphad and its cottage sixty yards away stood right by the road, it was still a lonely spot. The only building just within sight was the tiny Polharrow school which stood on the track up to Knocknalling House, the home of the Kennedy family.

It was about one o'clock as Nan neared the farmhouse that looked beyond the road to the banks of the river Ken. Unable to resist telling her friend Annie about her errand she decided to stop by before going on to Mary Timneys. Half of the front door was ajar and as she walked in she called Ann's name. The kitchen door, to the left down a short passageway, was closed. Nan could hear the sound of the cattle in the byre behind the house, they were noisy and unsettled as if they hadn't been attended to. She immediately knew something was wrong.

Still calling Ann's name Nan carefully pushed open the kitchen door for her eyes to be met by a scene of horror. Her friend was lying battered and senseless in pools of blood on the floor, her head horrifically bludgeoned, the scarlet and black worsted winter cap she routinely wore was lying, bloodsoaked, nearby.

"Oh dear me Ann what's ado?" Nan gasped hurrying for help, not from Mary Timney only a moment away but retracing her steps, running back along the turnpike road, down the track past the tiny school to the Porter's lodge at Knocknalling.

William Hannah was working in the fields three miles away with his brother when word came of the brutal attack on their sister. Lockhart had been digging drains since first light, and William had been moving stones to repair a dyke; hard, heavy work. It was a cold January Monday, the thirteenth, the first day of the old Scots new year. The day had begun for William in the dark when his tenant, Frank Timney sought him out where he was working in the byre, to borrow money. Light made an all too brief appearance in winter and the two brothers needed to make good use of their time, the short afternoon had started when a neighbour arrived with news. William had only recently added the fields at Greenloop to the eighteen acre farm after taking over the tenancy at the age of forty following the death of his mother the previous summer. Life was never easy working the land in this remote area of south west Scotland but in recent weeks William's quiet routine had been disrupted by dispute and argument between his twin sister Ann and their fiery tempered neighbour. And now this, an attack on his sister while she was quietly going about her Monday morning washing.

Leaving his older brother Lockhart to collect the tools, harness the pony back to the cart and return by road, William hurried back across country. The neighbour had warned William that his sister Ann was in a poor way and he arrived to find a small crowd gathered around his front door. Inside, the neighbours had lifted Ann into her bed but the severity of her wounds was clear to everyone. When the surgeon doctor, Andrew Jackson arrived William confided to him that he suspected foul play and he'd sent Lockhart to bring the police constable from New Galloway.

As William and Dr Jackson entered the room they could see several people were gathered in the small kitchen including Mary Timney, who was sitting by the fireplace, cradling her fractious child. The doctor began to do what he could for Ann, dressing her ghastly injuries. Soon the baby's crying became too much for William and he told Mary to go home. It was clear to Dr Jackson that that there was no hope of Ann making a recovery, she had sustained seven severe wounds to her head and three serious cuts to her face. The doctor whispered his fears to William, solemnly shaking his head as a deathly quiet now descended on the room.

At six o'clock John Robson, the police constable from New Galloway, arrived with the town's doctor, Alfred Millman, having been alerted an hour earlier by Lockhart Hannah to the fact that "Ann was lying at home in a dying state apparently from blows and other injuries she had received from some person or persons unknown". Most of the people keeping a vigil at Ann's bedside had their suspicions about who had committed this terrible crime. Despite the front door of the house opening out onto the turnpike road it was little frequented, especially in winter and no one had been seen travelling along it that morning other than the children on their way to school. The arguments that had recently disturbed the quiet routine and rhythm of William Hannah's life had been between his twin sister and her hot headed young neighbour though he never imagined that the squabbles could escalate into vicious violence. As Ann lay dying PC Robson walked the sixty yards to the tiny cottage rented by the Hannah's to Frank Timney, his wife and their four young children.

Frank had left that morning for his work as a road surface man, working away in Corsock about fourteen miles away and only returning on alternate Saturdays. PC Robson found twenty seven year old Mary fully dressed but in her bed; she quickly denied all knowledge of the brutal attack. The constable, who had taken the doctor's son and a driver with him, demanded to see Mary's clothes, making her change and hand them over immediately. He also searched the simple one room cottage although it was dark and smoky. Robson discovered a bundle of bloodstained clothes roughly hidden in the roof joists and a wooden beetle or mallet behind a meal barrel. Believing it had nothing to do with the case he replaced it and returned to the farmhouse with the bundle of clothes. At half past nine that night, surrounded by her family and friends from this close knit rural community, Ann died from her injuries. Apart from a few whispered words of "oh dear, oh dear" she never regained consciousness.

PC Robson immediately went straight to the Timney's cottage and arrested Mary for the murder of Ann Hannah despite her strenuous claims to innocence. Carrying her baby son, Mary gathered her daughters, nine year old Susan, Margaret, seven, and five year old Mary, little knowing that they would never be together in their home again. As they reached Dalry arrangements were made to leave the girls with their grandmother, before Mary, still clutching her baby son, was taken south on the start of a journey that would end only three months later on the gallows.

A sketch by Hugh Thomson from Highways and Byways in Galloway and Carrick. The Polharrow bridge can be seen on the left foreground with the school a little beyond that. In the far centre you can see the buildings of Carsphad Farm.

Two

"The accused has the character of being inordinately fond of tea."

News of Ann Hannah's savage murder travelled quickly through the small community and on the following day rumours began to circulate in the towns of south west Scotland that "a murder had been committed in the Glenkens."

The brutality of the attack on this quiet middle aged woman in her own home, a remote roadside farmhouse, was an enormous shock to the people not only of the nearby villages but throughout the country. Serious crime like this was rare and it had been more than thirty years since anyone had been charged and executed in the region known now as Dumfries and Galloway. One local newspaper, *The Dumfries Herald and Register*, announced that "the deed of bloody violence has caused a great sensation in the quiet and well-ordered district of Glenkens." But the rumours about the murder had already rippled beyond the south west and the ramifications of the case would resonate far further than the quiet valley of the River Ken.

Details of the deed were already being discussed in St John's Town of Dalry before Mary's husband heard of what had happened to his neighbour and his wife. Late on Tuesday morning, as his wife and son were being taken to the prison at Kirkcudbright, Frank Timney was told of her arrest by Dalry shoemaker John Reed. He'd found Frank working on the road at Corsock on the way to Dumfries. Frank immediately downed tools and left, retracing his long walk of the previous day.

Newspapers all over the United Kingdom soon carried reports of the attack, the Victorian public had become voracious readers of murder cases. But they would gape at the horror of the deed rather than be intrigued by the 'Carsphad' or 'Glenkens Murder' as it was being called. There was no need for a detective from Edinburgh, Glasgow or Scotland Yard in this case, the local police had made an arrest and they were not looking for anyone else. There was no mystery; this would not be an inspiration for a Wilkie Collin's novel as the genteel poisoning of the Madeleine Smith case in Glasgow had been five years earlier. No love letters, no hint of scandal beneath the veneer of a metropolitan middle class household that had so gripped the nation's salacious interest. [1] This was a blunt and brutal crime inflicted on a stout middle aged spinster by someone from the lower, peasant, class in an obscure, remote part of the country. But it was murder nonetheless, still a rare crime, especially in such a quiet farming community, and not only that but it was also the murder of one woman by another and that was definitely news.

Despite the remoteness of this cluster of small villages the editor of *The Dumfries Courier* immediately sent a reporter to St John's Town of Dalry where "all kinds of tales were told of the occurrence and how it had been occasioned." As the first of many column inches began to appear in print, it seemed as if the prejudices and suspicions of those people who had first pointed the police towards Mary Timney's tiny cottage were rolling out across the region. The editors of titles from Stranraer to Dumfries very quickly adopted a position on the case and no one was giving any benefit of the doubt to the young mother who had been arrested. There was little in the way of regulation, then, over what could be reported in cases of murder and what began as a fairly tame trickle of opinion in the twenty-fourth of January edition of *The Kirkcudbright Advertiser* soon became a torrent against Mary Timney.

"In external appearance the dwelling is in accordance with the humble but respectable position of the occupants: it is a one storeyed cottage with a slated roof and whitewashed walls, having a byre and stable attached, and stands close by and on the left hand side of the turnpike road leading from New Galloway to Carsphairn. The high road follows the windings of the river ken on its right bank on which Carsphad is situated, the house being separated from the river only by the high road and a small strip of meadow forming part of the farm. This meadow is occasionally flooded by the Ken and wood and other wreck brought down from the higher lands are sometimes left upon it. At a distance of fifty or sixty yards beyond the house there is a turn in the road – there is another cottage, of a meaner appearance, occupied by a roadman named Francis Timney and his wife and family. These were the Hannah's nearest neighbours. Half a mile nearer New Galloway than Carsphad and near to Polharrow Bridge, two thatched cottages stand close by the roadside, one of which is occupied by a labourer named George McLellan. Between these cottages and Carsphad are the gate and lodge of Knocknalling House which lies enbosomed in woods at a considerable distance to the left of the high road. There is very little traffic at any time on the bleak mountain road that threads the gloomy passes of the Kells and Carsphairn, but in winter the wayfarers are few and far between and the spot where the bloody deed occurred wears a solitary and unfrequented appearance."

Readers who enjoyed the lurid sensationalist stories of the popular 'penny dreadfuls' would soon be more than satisfied by the Carsphad case as the gruesome details began to emerge about the murder scene. It was reported that found beside the dying woman was "a large butcher's knife covered in blood which was supposed to have been used in the commission of the diabolical deed, her head being cut in several places in a frightful manner, one of the cuts being about five inches long. Besides the knife a blunt instrument also appeared to have been used, a piece of iron about two feet long, with a knob on it having been found with blood and a small portion of hair attached."

The rumours and whispers about what may or may not have happened on that Monday morning were widely reported as fact not speculation, including one piece of information which would be crucial in the case.

"From information received by investigation made on the spot," *The Wigtownshire Free Press* claimed, "it appears that about ten o'clock on Monday morning two girls going to school spoke to the deceased and that about half an hour afterwards Mrs Timney had gone down to Carsphad and returned shortly afterwards with her clothes covered in blood and a wooden mallet in her hand. This mallet must have been taken to the house of the deceased who had been washing near the door of the cottage and had been knocked down suddenly, there being no appearance of any struggle having taken place." *The Dumfries Courier* stated emphatically that Mary had been seen returning with 'tea and sugar and a bloodstained handkerchief around her neck." *The Dumfries Herald and Register* added that "she accounted to her own children for the blood on her dress by saying she had given a thumping to the deceased." Although it would emerge later that there had been no witnesses to the actual attack and the whole legal case hinged on circumstantial evidence, these lurid and highly speculative descriptions were being read and discussed by the public and, in all likelihood, the men who, just three months later, would make up the jury at Mary Timney's trial.

In the excitement and early confusion mistakes made in the reports only enhanced the horror of the whole situation. *The Kirkcudbright Advertiser*, for example, reported that Agnes McLellan was a 'girl'. "When the girl McLellan entered the kitchen," the reporter wrote, "she was amazed to see Ann lying on her face on the floor, speechless, motionless and bareheaded, the woollen cap that she had been wearing lying at a little distance. It is a significant circumstance that the girl McLellan instead of going there [Timney's cottage] hastened in the opposite direction to the Knocknalling porter lodge a full quarter mile from Carsphad."

Although Agnes McLellan, middle aged by Victorian standards at age thirty nine, was clearly not a 'girl', *The Dumfries Herald and Register* even referred to her as a 'little girl'. What the papers had yet to uncover was that key to the case were a number of girls who were very young, including two of Mary's daughters, who were actually the only witnesses of any real value to the authorities. Initially unaware of this, the reporters continued to highlight the horrific murder scene and the assumed guilt of Mary Timney. *The Kirkcudbright Advertiser* reported that on examining the head of the deceased, Dr Jackson had found it to present "a fearful spectacle; the scalp was cut in several places which, apparently, had been a work of some time, and the back of the head had been completely smashed in" adding that the doctor had seen fit to question Mary: "Had she heard any noise or seen any one about the place to which she said no saying 'she had been in bed all the forenoon with a sore head.'"

As if this report wasn't damning enough, the journalist went on to make more claims that would further shock his readers; money had been discovered which Mary claimed she had gained by selling a pig and which she had concealed from her husband, but was suspected to have come from the Hannah's house. The police had discovered oatcakes and a cloth containing a mixture of tea and sugar hidden in the bottom of a chest. "It must be mentioned in this place," the reporter emphasised," that the accused has the character of being inordinately fond of tea."

This last statement initially seems somewhat absurd but research by Dr Helen O'Connell of Durham University sheds light on the message behind the accusation. She discovered that pamphlets published in the nineteenth century by middle and upper class social reformers condemned poor women for drinking tea as they were seen to be squandering their time and their limited resources, drawing them away from their primary duty to their family and home. "Tea was thought to threaten traditional ways – an affront to the virtues of frugality and restraint – which underpinned rural Irish culture," Dr O'Connell stated in her paper published in Literature and History.[2] Tea was considered to be an exotic substance with potentially habit forming properties as it came from China and it could lead to "lavish, irresponsible behaviour." Poor women who drank tea were viewed as being as irresponsible as whisky drinkers. Sugar was also a target of the middle class campaigners due to its association with slavery. The pamphlets were widespread in Ireland but also produced in England suggesting that the concerns about tea and sugar consumption amongst peasant women were widely held. The strong links between the south west of Scotland and Ireland, including the large seasonal influx of migrant workers, make it highly likely that these views on tea drinking were familiar to people in the region. In light of this research, the seemingly innocuous sentence about Mary's apparent fondness for tea takes on a much more accusatory tone that the community would have understood.

The claim that Mary had sold a pig and kept the money from her husband would also have been viewed as the most appalling behaviour in a wife. Mary was being clearly portrayed in the worst possible terms; she had betrayed the Victorian view of femininity by committing a violent act and she was being condemned as a failure in her womanly and wifely duties. A picture was being painted by the press of Mary Timney as a violent, deceitful, callous woman who had murdered her poor neighbour in an horrific, premeditated and unprovoked attack for nothing more than a few coins and a handful of tea and sugar. It was a depiction based on hearsay as was some of the case being compiled by the authorities. What some witnesses had to say was little more than local gossip but Mary was doing little to help her own case. Her denials and increasingly wild statements would, in the end, go a long way towards condemning her. "One point tells strongly against the accused," *The Kirkcudbright Advertiser* stated," she swore she'd not been wearing a tartan dress but at least two witnesses saw her wearing it."

Three

"Sober, moral and religious with sound and healthy constitutions."

Although Mary had been accused of the murder of her neighbour, on the night of her arrest Constable Robson felt able to leave her in the company of his wife, also called Mary. The two women sat together as the policeman travelled to Kirkcudbright to alert the Chief Constable and get advice on how to proceed. On Mary's arrival during the final hour of the Monday night both women exchanged pleasantries before sitting and talking over a cup of tea. For Mary the police house in the High Street at New Galloway, now aptly called Copper Cottage, would have been very comfortable especially compared to the alternative accommodation for prisoners – the gaol, a building used to imprison debtors and petty criminals. As the two women talked Mary admitted to disagreements with Ann Hannah but continued to claim she was as innocent as her son sitting on her knee.[1]

The following morning after receiving Constable Robson's news, a number of officials made the journey north from the county town of Kirkcudbright to begin the investigation into the death of Ann Hannah. Mr Gordon, the Procurator Fiscal, Mr Hamilton, the Steward Clerk, John Johnstone, the Chief Constable for the Stewartry of Kirkcudbrightshire, and three police officers were accompanied by Dr John Shand who was to carry out the post mortem examination at Dalry assisted by the local doctors Millman and Jackson. The officials, who were joined by the minister and Justice of the Peace for Kells, the

Reverend Dr James Maitland, would spend two days at Carsphad and Polharrow School interviewing twenty five witnesses. At the same time Mary and her infant son were taken south along the same turnpike road, little knowing that she was leaving the Glenkens for the last time.

Both Mary and her neighbours, the Hannahs, had been born and brought up in the area. Despite *The Kirkcudbright Advertiser* referring to the "bleak mountain road" and the "gloomy passes", the Glenkens has great charm though it is still described as the forgotten part of Scotland due to its remoteness. Running south from the border with Ayrshire, along the path of the river Ken, the Glenkens includes the villages of Carsphairn, Dalry, Balmaclellan and the Royal Burgh of New Galloway encompassing the parishes of Dalry and Kells. There are wild, high hills and moorland, contrasting with a wide flood plain further down the glen, a spectacular backdrop for the visitor but a hard landscape for the local people especially in the nineteenth century. Farming was at the heart of the lives of most of the people of the area. *The Statistical Account of 1839*, revised in 1844 by Rev Maitland, described the local people as being "sober, moral and religious with sound and healthy constitutions. The food of the peasantry is the same as in other parts of the south-west of Scotland, chiefly oatmeal and potatoes. There is a considerable consumption of bacon and mutton ham."[2]

It is apparent in his book *Highways and Byways in Galloway and Carrick* written in 1916, that the Rev C H Dick was very taken with area and the village of Dalry in particular. "You come to a part of the way" he wrote, "where it makes a series of undulations, and at the top of every rise, as you look across the masses of foliage embowering the river in the depths of the glen, you see the cottages and gardens of Dalry climbing skywards about a mile away. If it is late on a summer evening you will notice also how the little white walls retain the light of the dying day while all the surrounding details are sunk in shade. Even when one is on the top of the Kells range, seven or eight miles away, a small splash of white on the east side of the Ken valley enables one to say 'There is

Dalry.' Close at hand the village has a dazzling effect in full sunshine for the inhabitants vie with one another in glorifying their dwellings, not only growing flowers in strips of soil and training the creepers up the fronts, but painting or whitewashing the walls every year and your eye is constrained to seek relief sometimes in the meadows and plantations on the other side of the glen."

It is possible that at times in her short life Mary Timney had also been able to enjoy the landscape that so delighted the minister half a century later but as the wife of a man scraping a living from casual labour and the mother of four living children, poverty probably proved to be a very different prism through which to see what the Reverend Dick later described as a dazzling whitewashed idyll.

Mary was the eldest of four illegitimate children born to her unmarried parents. There appears to be no register of her birth in the baptismal records but the birth of her two younger sisters in 1836 is recorded, possibly because one of the twins was not expected to live. The record states that "William Reid and Margaret Corson in Clachan had two illegitimate children baptised December eleventh 1836 called Margaret and Susan." How long Margaret survived is not known but only Susan appears with her sister Mary and younger brother, William, in the first census of 1841. The three Reid children lived in Dalry with their twenty five year old mother Margaret Carson or Corson, seventy five year old grandparents James, a joiner and his wife Mary, along with their twenty year old aunt Jean. The only William Reid recorded in the area is a lead miner living at the Woodhead mine just outside Carsphairn. The fact that the father of the children appears not to have lived with the family and by 1851 had disappeared from the scene, makes the young miner a likely candidate to be Mary's parent. During the later controversy of Mary's court case there would be rumours claiming Mary was Irish, though on her mother's side the family were from Dalry, certainly for the previous two generations. These remarks could simply be a reference to the fact that her husband Frank Timney was Irish, or a reference to his

Catholicism, but it is highly likely that William Reid was also an Irish Catholic. Certainly he had left the area by 1851 when the census records that Mary's mother was by then living with a much older man. Whether Margaret Corson or Carson, names frequently changed spelling, ever married either William Reid or Samuel Good is not clear, there is certainly no mention of a marriage to either man in the parish records. Farm labourer Samuel Good, Mary's step father, was thirty years older than Margaret. As the Good family of Carsphairn dated back more than hundred years she probably regarded him as a safer bet than the itinerant miner William Reid.

The 1851 census, taken at the end of March, found the family living at Polharrow in the parish of Kells, just a few miles north of Dalry but to the west of the River Ken. Margaret was listed as Samuel's wife but irregular marriages, an exchange of promises before witnesses or proof of marriage by cohabitation and repute, were common in Scotland. When their daughter Jane, born in 1849, later gave evidence during the murder investigation, she described her parents as "living together and I live with them." Of significance, though, is the fact that this census records the presence of a lodger in the Good household where nineteen year old Mary and her fifteen year old sister live. He was an Irish farm labourer by the name of Francis Timoney who at forty was the same age as the girls' mother.

Frank Timoney was, not uncommonly, illiterate, he marked the register for the births of his children with a cross. Not surprisingly the spelling of his name changes often in the public records and the spelling Timney first appears only after Mary's arrest. Mary could read and write so perhaps just assumed the name was spelt as it was pronounced. It is possible that the names Timmony and Timney were Galloway colloquialisms for the name Timothy, though the name, in its various spellings, does appear in parts of Ireland, particularly the northern counties. Frank was from County Donegal. Migrant Irish labourers played a key role in the agricultural life of Scotland, especially the south west, for many years. Due to the poverty and poor state of health of many of the Irish who travelled to Scotland, they tended to settle near the point of arrival and as a result Wigtownshire and Kirkcudbrightshire had substantial Irish populations by 1841.[3] Some people regarded the Irish as "drunken, idle, uncivilised and undermining the moral fibre of Scottish society" and they were regularly criticised in the press, the pulpits and on the streets though the accusations were often more to do with poverty than ethnicity.[4] This attitude towards the Irish or Scotch Irish goes some way to explain the view of Mary that was presented in the pre-trial press reports.

It is not clear how long Frank had lived with the Goods or how Mary, later described even by her critics as a not unattractive young woman, came to be married to a man who was lame and more than twenty years her senior. Yet, on the tenth of June 1851 Mary, who may have been either nineteen years old or seventeen given that she gives her age ten years later as twenty seven, married Francis Tymony at the church in St John's Town of Dalry. Five children followed, Susan born early the following year, a son who didn't survive infancy, Margaret in July 1855, Mary three years later and John born in the December of 1860.

When Mary was pregnant with John, the family moved from Polharrow into a one room cottage a little further along the road from Carsphad farmhouse. Farm worker accommodation was a far cry in the middle of the nineteenth century from the bucolic scene described by the Rev Dick during his tour of the region sixty years later. An architectural review carried out in 1860 reported that the upper portion of Kirkcudbrightshire, the Glenkens, lagged behind other areas of the country in carrying out modernising improvements to agricultural property.[5]

"There we still find cottages built of dry stone," the report read, "the walls differing from a dyke in no other way than in having some lime thrown in a slap-dash way in the interstices on the outside. Drainage there is none, notwithstanding which, the houses are often built in a hollow some feet beneath the road which runs in front of them, and, as the floors are composed of nothing but natural soil, they are in a very sloppy state in winter. A foot-square window is in many instances the only source of light, if we except the door, which, to prevent suffocation by smoke, is usually left open. Numerous houses have no grates, the peats being built up on the floor, beneath where a hole in the roof does – or rather we should say, is intended to, but does not - do duty as a chimney. As might be expected, the furniture of such houses is usually in keeping with the character of the accommodation they afford. A box-bed, and one composed of slabs from the saw mill; a chest or two for clothes, three or four stools, a couple of home-made chairs, and a clock of the description there known as a 'wag-at-the-wa' are often all the plenishing. The inmates are not to blame, for any better would be sadly out of place, and glued articles would be destroyed in a week in such hovels. In these wretched dwellings there can be little or no real comfort."

From evidence given during the murder investigation this description of the typical farm worker's cottage almost exactly matches the tiny roadside accommodation the Timney family moved into before December 1860 when John was born. The cottage was leased to them by the tenant farmer, Margaret Hannah who had taken on the eighteen acre farm after the death of husband Robert, age forty-six, in 1833. The farm would have been typical of the area, growing barley, oats and turnips with a small herd of black cattle and at least one pig. "There are a great number of pigs. Almost every cottager has one to fatten for their own use or for market," the Rev Maitland reported in the 1844 *Statistical Review*. The 1841 census records Margaret Hannah living at Carsphad with her ninety one year old mother, Ann McClacherty, and her daughter Ann. The Hannah name was sometimes given as Hannay and it appears this way in at least one census and in the written evidence taken during the murder investigation. Ann's name also changed spelling, sometimes being written as Anne or Annie. There were four other children, Walter, twins James and Lockhart and William, Ann's twin. Although James certainly returned to the area, dying in 1905 age eighty seven at Knockman farm to the north east of Dalry, there is no mention of him in the investigation evidence or in the 1861 census of the area, and it can only be assumed that he was living away. Walter and Lockhart moved to Wales as young men, probably looking for work as the small farm at Carsphad would not support the whole family. Although Lockhart returned to the Glenkens some time in the late 1850s, in 1843 he was working as a draper in Cardiff where he married Ann Jones, the wedding announcement appearing in *The Wigtownshire Free Press*.[6] Walter remained in Glamorganshire working as the landlord of the Albion pub in Aberdare until his death age seventy two in 1888.

Lockhart was a troubled man and after his return to Carsphad he spent some months at the relatively new Southern Asylum, part of the Crichton Royal Hospital in Dumfries, his treatment paid for by the parish. After his discharge he continued to come and go from the farm; William admitted to the murder investigators that there had been at least one dispute over a horse between Lockhart and Ann that caused his brother to leave home. From his statements during the investigation it is clear that Lockhart had a friendly relationship with the Timneys, particularly Frank, and was often to be found sitting at the family's fireside of an evening.

The two cottages were for many years the very picture of rural life, the smaller building inhabited by a series of families working on the land, the McGills, for example, where the father was employed as a sheep driver. It is more than likely that when the Timneys moved into the cottage Frank was working, at times, for the Hannahs along with other farms in the area. On John's birth record Frank described himself as a farm labourer but in the census of the following spring he had become a road surface man. He may have been forced to find alternative work, perhaps due to the many changes happening in agriculture, or because of Lockhart's return from the asylum. It seems that for some time the two families lived relatively harmoniously with each other, Margaret frequently helped Mary who struggled to keep her children fed on what little her husband earned. She perhaps saw something of herself in the young mother, but after Margaret's death in June 1861 there was a significant change. Ann made no secret of the fact that she disliked Mary and she reduced the support given for so long by her mother before not only refusing all help but pressing her brother William to throw the family out of the cottage. During the winter of 1861 the relationship between Ann and Mary deteriorated to such an extent that it would lead to both of their deaths, one at the hands of the other, the other at the hands of the State.

Detail from the OS Kirkcudbrightshire 6":1 mile First Edition Sheet 15.

Four

"In her sober senses and exceedingly cool and collected."

Things moved apace during the days following Ann Hannah's death. Witnesses were interviewed initially in the Polharrow schoolroom, the statements written down by the Reverand Maitland in his capacity not only as minister to the parish but also a Justice of the Peace. The Kirkcudbright doctor, John Shand, carried out a post mortem assisted by Dr Millman and Dr Jackson who had attended to Ann as she lay dying. On Saturday Ann Hannah's funeral was held at the parish church in Dalry. The newspapers mentioned the event briefly, their focus on the alleged murderess rather than the victim, and it was reported that it had been well attended by the local community. For forty years Ann had lived and slept in the same small kitchen as her mother and only seven months after Margaret's death the two were joined again in the family plot. The inscription on the headstone, which would eventually bear the names of the whole family, did not mention the dreadful circumstances of Ann's sudden death.

Mary Timney, meanwhile, had been taken to the county gaol at Kirkcudbright, a relatively new building in the centre of the town, built after a period of major prison reform in 1839. Before that imprisonment had been a rare punishment, most people being banished, transported or executed. It was housed in a four storey tower building just across from the Tolbooth, where criminals and debtors had previously been incarcerated, and next door to the court house.

On arrival at the prison Mary was searched by Agnes, the wife of the superintendent Thomas Richardson. Mary had only a few coppers in her possession and Agnes found that both Mary and her baby were very cold and allowed them to sit near the fire. Mary continued to protest her innocence to anyone who would listen though she had begun to admit that she had been down to the farmhouse that morning where she and Ann had "had words." She told Agnes that she'd felt unwell and had sent for her mother.[1] It is impossible to know if Mary was simply confused, given everything that had happened in the previous twenty four hours or whether she was deliberately formulating the preposterous version of events that she would later reveal to the investigators. Certainly the newspapers would regard her words as those of a devious and immoral woman.

As the first statements were given, the Chief Constable of the Stewartry began a full search of the Timney's cottage, the first in daylight. Despite the fact that the family were desperately poor and owned nothing of value, Mary had locked the door when the family was taken away, entrusting the key to nine year old Susan when she was parted from the girls at Dalry. John Johnstone had drafted in twenty nine year old William Donaldson, the police constable for Dalbeattie, a town twenty two miles to the south beyond Castle Douglas, and James Richardson, the officer from Carsphairn, to help with the investigation. The fact that the Chief Constable led the investigation and carried out the search himself is an indication of just how few police officers there were at the time. The fledgeling Stewartry force dated from 1849, established just over a decade after Dumfries, the first in the region. Hours were long, wages low and disciplinary codes rigorously enforced. Each officer had to make a deposit of ten shillings with the Chief Constable before being issued with his equipment which he was expected to return on retirement.

As rural officers in a relatively new police force none of the constables would have dealt with anything like the 'Glenkens Murder'. The previous execution in south west Scotland under the 'Bloody Code' for crimes punishable by death, had been more than a generation earlier when in 1826 James McManus was hanged in Dumfries for assault and robbery. [2] The Victorian crime statistics make it clear that homicide was not a serious problem, from the middle of the century the incidence had been declining and the majority of people brought before the courts were young men guilty of petty crime. [3] This was certainly the case in the Glenkens. In the the *Old Statistical Review* carried out in Scotland between 1791 and 1799, the minister for Dalry, the Rev Mr Alexander McGowan commented: "It is remarkable that even the most idle, dissipated and worthless part of the inhabitants are not destitute of all those good qualities which distinguish the rest. Scarcely any of them, for a long period have been convicted of capital crimes though there have been a few, especially in the village, who are said to be addicted to fraud, pilfering, lying, evil speaking and several other immoralities." [4]

Given the inexperience of the police it is not surprising that John Robson had replaced the wooden beetle he'd found behind the meal barrel believing it had nothing to do with the case, after all two weapons had been found at the scene of the crime that were bloodstained and had obviously been used in the attack. The police searched the cottage again thoroughly, and in daylight, on the fifteenth of January. William Donaldson said in his statement that the cottage was "very bare of furnishings" the occupants were clearly "very poor." He described the building as having one window and bare joists in the roof apart from one area above the beds where there was some boarding. The box beds, which ran down the centre of the room creating a storage space to one side, had mattresses or ticks which were "common ticking filled with chaff" though he noted that the sheets were clean. To one side there were "turnips, straw and old some old pots". Of interest is the fact that PC Donaldson stated that he measured the distance between the farmhouse and the cottage with a tape, it was one hundred and seventy-eight feet or fifty-nine yards from door to door.

James Richardson noticed that the family had a clock, a pair of clogs and beneath the press (shelves or a dresser) he discovered the wooden beetle PC Robson had found on the night of Mary Timney's arrest. Robson was certain that he had replaced it behind the meal barrel, although he thought that it had been wet the house was so dark and smoky he could not see it clearly. The beetle had obviously been moved and an attempt made to hide it after Robson left with the bundle of clothes. In the daylight the police officers believed that the beetle was bloodstained.[5]

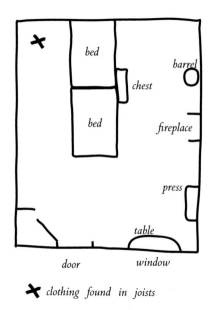

✖ clothing found in joists

Diagram of the Timney's cottage.

On his way north to Dalry the previous day, the Chief Constable had met Frank Timney at New Galloway and arranged for him and his three daughters to be conveyed to Carsphad to be examined for the precognition, the legal process of gathering evidence. On their arrival at Polharrow School he showed the beetle to Timney and the children and the newspapers reported that they had all identified it as belonging to the family, the girls revealing that they had been in the habit of using it as a doll. As there is no statement from Frank Timney in the precognition papers it is impossible to verify the newspaper claims but there is a document in the archive at Broughton House in Kirkcudbright. In this statement Frank says that he was shown a batt by the legal authorities but he could not swear that it was theirs.[6] He admitted that they had such an implement which they used to mash turnips but he thought it was a different one and theirs was still at home in the cottage.

The police remained convinced that the mallet had been used by Mary in the attack on Ann and it was taken, along with the knife, the poker, the bundle discovered in the roof joists and the clothes removed from Mary by the matron, Mrs Clark, at Kirkcudbright gaol, personally by the Chief Constable to Edinburgh to be scientifically examined by Dr Douglas Mclagan of Heriot Row. The results of his experiments would prove to be vital to the prosecution's evidence. Before leaving for Edinburgh, Mr Johnstone attended Mary's first declaration before the Steward Substitute of Kirkcudbright, William Hyacinth Dunbar who had "duly admonished and warned the accused." Judicial examinations took place before a magistrate whose duty was to protect the prisoner from any unfair or oppressive questioning as the prisoner, at this stage, was not allowed to have any legal advice. Any statement from the prisoner had to be made freely and voluntarily and not due to threats or promises. The magistrate had to be satisfied that the prisoner was in sound and sober senses. Mr Johnstone wrote in his evidence that Mary had been in her "sober senses and exceedingly cool and collected."

Five

"The chief witnesses are five little girls."

Although the Victorian broadsheet newspapers did not have the banner headlines we associate with the modern tabloid press, within the columns of print the reporters were just as graphic in their coverage of the case, if not more so. They were not under the legal restrictions that apply to the reporting of crime today and there was little effort made to present a balanced picture of the event. All the editors claimed to have their own people 'on the spot' but in reality it is likely, given the similarities in the articles, that all the information was coming from *The Dumfries Courier's* man. Several people in the community appeared to have plenty to say about Mary Timney but none of it good. Details were beginning to emerge of disputes and bad feeling between the two women. In the eighteenth of January edition, *The Dumfries Standard* reported: "The deceased woman and the accused appear to have been on very bad terms with each other and the latter was heard to say that she would go to Hannah's house and leave a corpse some day. A female who was visiting the accused when the deceased was standing nearby speaking to two men, was called on by the accused to take notice of Ann Hannah, the former adding the words 'I think she is ower fond o' the men. My man gangs in sometimes and sits a bit when her brithers are away but I'll dae for her yet. I'll gang and leave her a corpse some morning.' The visitor thereupon told her 'to use her tongue and hands as she liked but to take no weapon.'"

Despite there being no witnesses to the attack, the *Standard's* reporter felt able to give an almost blow by blow account of what, he claimed, had happened. "It is considered likely that the deceased after being severely struck by a wooden mallet from behind, was able to make an attempt at defending herself with a poker and that the latter had been wrestled from her and she had then received repeated blows upon her head which was the immediate cause of her death. The poor woman had possibly put her arms up in a vain attempt to protect her head as they have been beaten dreadfully as if with a poker." He then added, somewhat as an afterthought having been carried away by his own prose and imagination, that "much of this, however, is mere conjecture. The evidence against Timney, it is right to add, is, though strong, entirely circumstantial and she declares she is entirely innocent of the murder."

The 'on the spot reporter' was clearly very good at his job as the description of Ann Hannah's injuries very accurately represented the post mortem report later presented at the trial and the 'female's' account would also be repeated in court, so someone involved in the precognition process was being somewhat indiscreet. The presentation of theories as fact continued in *The Dumfries Courier*. "It was evident," the report read, "that the first and most violent blow had been struck while the deceased was bending over her work, there were wounds and bruising to the arms and wrists as if the poor woman had raised her hands to protect her head and the weight of blows had descended on them." The reporter went on, giving full vent to his imaginative theory, though failing to point out that it was entirely speculative, "she [Ann Hannah] succeeded in reaching a table at the other side of the kitchen where the knife lay but that she had succumbed to repeated blows, when the knife would have fallen from her nerveless grasp; a supposition borne out to some extent by the bloody marks found on chairs and tables as well as on the floor of that part of the kitchen furthest from the window."

Almost all the reporting on the case condemned Mary – even before she was charged. *The Scotsman* did give her some benefit of the doubt. In the twenty-second of January edition Mary was described as "27, black haired of active habits and not unprepossessing appearance. The deceased was a powerful, strongly built woman with whom, in a fair encounter, the other would have had no chance whatsoever. It is believed that the occupants were about to receive notice to quit at Whit Sunday as the two women were often quarrelling." Two days later *The Dumfries Herald and Register* described Mary as "a Scotch woman and rather good looking and active in her habits." Yet it went on to say "there are unfavourable reports as to her temper and moral dispositions, but there is a heavy pressure of circumstantial evidence against her, it is well to refrain from circulating loose statements to her prejudice." Despite this last sentence the *Herald and Register*, a newspaper regarded as having the closest ties to the religious authorities of the Dumfries Burgh, ignored its own advice and surmised about the attack itself. "From the appearance of the scene of blood and as she was a strong woman and to be subdued easily, the immediate supposition was that she had been stunned first of all by an unexpected blow on the head while bending over the tub in the act of washing clothes."

Before the end of January newspaper readers across Scotland had been led to believe that Mary was an immoral, ill tempered woman who had launched a merciless, unprovoked attack on her neighbour as she was quietly going about her domestic chores. Mary didn't need any more bad press but her own attempts to explain what had happened on that Monday morning only served to exacerbate the situation. Mary appeared before the advocate steward-substitute at Kirkcudbright, William Hyacinth Dunbar and given two opportunities to make a statement about the murder, on the fourteenth and seventeenth of January and then again on the fourth of February when she offered a further explanation. In her first declaration Mary accounted for the tea and sugar found mixed together in a cloth by saying that she had sent her daughter Susan to Dalry on the previous Saturday to buy it. In the second she was presented with the wooden mallet which she denied had ever belonged to her, was ever seen by her or had ever been in her house. At her instigation she appeared again before William Dunbar and the papers soon learned what she had said. They published the news that not only had Mary, after three weeks in prison, continued to deny murdering her neighbour, insisting that she'd been ill in bed, but she had an extraordinary explanation for how bloodstains came to be on her tartan dress, the dress she denied having worn despite evidence to the contrary from numerous witnesses, including her own children. Her preposterous story would further blacken her name and reputation – in an elaborate tale she blamed her own mother for the brutal attack on Ann Hannah.

A view from The Tolbooth, Kirkcudbright with the four storey prison tower rising above the buildings to the left.

All Mary's claims were easily refuted; every grocer in Dalry denied having seen Susan Timney on the Saturday in question. The poor child was even taken round to each store to see if the shopkeepers recognised her, and a large number of people were able to verify that

Margaret Good or Corson, Mary's mother, had been at home washing all day. Was it wickedness or desperation? The writers and readers of the newspapers certainly felt it was the former and there was further outraged condemnation of Mary as a "savage and implacable monster." With the forces of the law, the hostility of her local community who were queuing up to condemn her, the weight of the media and public feeling all building against her there seemed to be little hope of a fair trial for the young woman.

Yet the legal team preparing the case against her were still concerned that all the evidence was circumstantial. A letter to Andrew Murray, the Crown Agent in Edinburgh from the Procurator Fiscal, Mr Gordon, included in the precognition papers, illustrates that they were well aware of the difficulties of the case. "The chief witnesses are five little girls averaging from seven to twelve years of age, two of them respectively being daughters of the accused. The latter two have been seen frequently and they have never once deviated from their first statements."

From another letter amongst the documents it is clear they were anxious to see Dr Mclagan's report before Mary was indicted to Dumfries, only too aware that other than his conclusions, the case rested on the testimony of "the woman's own children." The Procurator Fiscal wrote to Andrew Murray on the twenty-first of January, "I am directed by the substitute to intimate (there being no doubt but that the above party [Mary Timney] has committed murder that the most important evidence will be given by two of the Pannel's [a term in Scot's Law meaning the accused] children respectively aged ten and seven years and who are living with the father and grandmother. They are both very intelligent and at present tell a plain straightforward story but they may be tampered with and give confused evidence at trial when put on the witness box." [1]

Despite their fears it appears, from evidence given at the trial, that the children remained at their grandmother's. The baby, who Mary had been allowed to keep with her on her arrest, was taken from her after her formal committal on February fourth. Mary was taken to Dumfries in readiness for her trial which had been set for the 8th of April. It would be the first case heard at the Spring session of the Circuit-Court of Justiciary within the Criminal Court House in the town. The indictment is a sobering document.

It begins:

> *MARY REID or TIMNEY, now or lately prisoner in the prison of Kirkcudbright, you are Indicted and Accused, at the instance of JAMES MONCREIFF, Esquire, Her Majesty's Advocate for Her Majesty's interest: THAT ALBEIT, by the laws of this and of every well-governed realm, MURDER is a crime of an heinous nature, and severely punishable: YET TRUE IT IS AND OF VERITY, that you the said Mary Reid or Timney are guilty of the said crime, actor, or art and part : IN SO FAR AS, on the 13th day of January 1862, or on one or other of the days of that month, or of December immediately preceding, or of February immediately following, within or near the house situated at or near Carsphad, in the parish of Kells, and Stewartry of Kirkcudbright, then and now or lately occupied by the William Hannah, labourer, also now or lately residing there, you the said Mary Reid or Timney did, wickedly and feloniously, attack and assault the now deceased Ann Hannah, sister or, and then or lately before residing with, the said William Hannah and Lockhart Paterson Hannah, in the said house at or near Carsphad aforesaid, and did with a poker, or piece of iron, and with a wooden beetle or mallet, or with one or other of them, or with some other lethal weapon or weapons to the prosecutor unknown, strike the said Ann Hannah several or one or more severe blows on or about the head, face and other parts of her person, whereby the said Ann Hannah was cut, bruised, and wounded, on or about the head, face, and other parts of her person, and whereby her skull was fractured: by all which, or part thereof, the said Ann Hannah was thus murdered by you the said Mary Reid or Timney."*

It is worth noting that the blood stained knife found at the scene along with the poker, is not individually mentioned in the extensive list of items. The document continues, going on to itemise the evidence not only the poker and the mallet but each article of clothing, including the tartan dress and a child's pinafore and nightdress and also "a piece of cloth, containing tea and sugar," "seven or thereby pieces of oatcake" and a "a tin case, containing tea." It then lists each of the fifty four witnesses gathered to testify against Mary including her children, her mother, her stepfather and stepsister, her neighbours, and people she had thought of as acquaintances if not friends. The indictment states:

"ALL WHICH, or part thereof, being found proven by the verdict of an Assize, or admitted by the judicial confession of you the said Mary Reid or Timney before the Lord Justice-General, Lord Justice-Clerk, and Lords Commissioners of Justiciary, in a Circuit-court of Justiciary to be holden by them, or by any one or more of their number, within the burgh of Dumfries in the month of April, in this present year 1862, you the said Mary Reid or Timney OUGHT to be punished with the pains of law, to deter others committing the like crimes in all time coming."

Mary signed every page of each declaration, these signatures from the first and last, made three weeks later, illustrate the strain of her imprisonment.

Six

"She seemed scarcely to realise the dreadful circumstances of her position."

The old Dumfries gaol or prison had been on the east side of the High street, but it was not a building suitable for its purpose, the prisoners frequently escaped. It was partly destroyed after a poor vagrant woman, charged with pilfering a pair of stockings, accidentally started a fire in her cell after asking for a small bit of candle to light the gloom. Although it was repaired, the authorities resolved to build a new prison though the site chosen was unpopular due to its location in Buccleuch Street, regarded as a genteel part of town. It contained eight cells for criminals and four small rooms but this in turn was replaced in 1851, following the prison reforms of 1839–40, by a larger structure capable of holding up to sixty inmates. It was to this prison, positioned on the corner of Buccleuch Street and what was then called St David's Street, now known as Irish Street, that Mary Timney was taken to await trial. The court building was then on the opposite side of the street to the prison and there was an underground tunnel running between the two.

Dumfries, in the east of the region, is the largest town in south west Scotland. In the nineteenth century it was still a busy port with a regular market and a thriving tweed industry. The High Court of Justiciary was the highest court authority in Scotland and it had a system of assize courts in four circuits, west, east, south and north which sat twice a year. It was Mary's misfortune that the judge who travelled to Dumfries in April to hear her trial at the spring assizes was the notorious Lord Deas;

"an impressive figure, deep set eyes, a noble nose, luxurious side whiskers and a mouth that turned down very decidedly at the corners. He was so inclined towards capital punishment that he was known in the Court of Sessions in Edinburgh as Lord Death."[1] Born in Fife in 1804 George Deas was called to the Scottish bar in 1828 and in 1840 was appointed advocate depute. He later became the Solicitor General of Scotland after which he was created a lord ordinary of the court of session with the judicial title of Lord Deas. In 1854 he was made a Lord Commissioner of Justiciary and was knighted four years later. According to the *Dictionary of National Biography* he "spoke with a broad Scotch accent." [2]

Lord Deas travelled by train from Edinburgh arriving at Lockerbie station where he was met with some ceremony by James Gordon, the

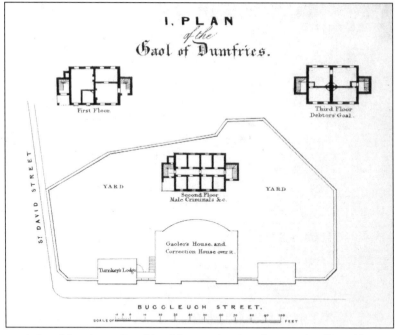

A plan of the prison at Dumfries. Mary was imprisoned, executed and buried here.

Provost of Dumfries, and the town's magistrates. He was then escorted to the Commerical Inn in Dumfries where the staff of the militia were drawn up to receive him. The Commercial Inn, later the County Hotel, once stood near the fountain in the town's High Street, and although it was demolished in the 1980s something of the facade was kept and incorporated into the replacement building. During the evening before the trial, as Lord Deas had a meeting with Provost Gordon, Mary would have been introduced to her advocate, Hugh Cowan, for the first time. Legal aid did not exist in 1862 but Mary would have been provided with some advice through the 'poor roll' whereby an advocate would volunteer his services on what would now be called a pro bono system. It is unlikely in a town the size of Dumfries that there would be any advocates living in permanent residence so Mr Cowan probably arrived along with the rest of the court personnel. She had been allocated a legal writer from Castle Douglas, Richard Hewat, who had asked Mr Cowan to represent Mary shortly before the trial. Amongst the precognition papers are letters sent from Mr Hewat after the trial complaining that he had not been properly reimbursed for all his expenses.

The Dumfries Standard reported that on Tuesday April eighth, the first day of the Spring Assizes, a procession led by the Provost, magistrates and militia accompanied Lord Deas to the Court House in Buccleuch Street where he took his seat on the bench at ten o'clock in the morning. "The court was densely crowded, the circumstances of the Carsphad murder in the lists causing extraordinary excitement in the town and throughout Galloway." *The Kirkcudbright Advertiser* said that court room had been crowded from an early hour with "hundreds waiting for admission during the day." Other papers claimed that "for some hours before the Assizes opened, Buccleuch Street was almost entirely blocked up by a large crowd besieging the front and side entrances to the Courthouse for admittance." Any bystanders hoping to catch a glimpse of Mary Timney would have been disappointed as she would have been taken to court through the underground passage.

The officials assembled; Mr Aitken and Mr Hamilton attended as Clerks of the Court, Mr Adam Gifford acted as the Advocate Depute and the counsel present for the prisoner were Mr Hugh Cowan, Mr Thomas McKie instructed by Richard Hewat, writer of Castle Douglas. The Kirkcudbright Advertiser listed the jury, which in Scotland has fifteen members;

James Church, farmer, Tower of Sark,
William Hunter, farmer, Drumfedling,
Hugh Dalziel, draper, Thornhill,
James Brydon, farmer, Moodlaw,
William Rae, farmer, Gateslack,
Samuel McKeand, Braeside Cottage, Gatehouse,
Andrew Irving, ironmonger, Annan,
Robert Proudfoot, merchant, Minnyhive,
Robert Milligan, innkeeper, Lockerbie,
Alexander McMichan, farmer, Upper Drumwall,
William McMiken, farmer, Culreoch,
William Miller, farmer, Lakehead,
Anthony Heron, draper, Annan,
William Hunter, farmer, Sundaywell
Walter Fergusson, farmer, Hillend.[3]

Of course the right to a trial by a jury of peers was not really true for women as at this time only men were able to serve. Mary was to be judged not by her peers but only by men of property and the majority at her trial were farmers. *The Dumfries Standard* described Mary as exhibiting "no trace of feeling, her face wearing an impassive aspect, and the expression being vacant and insensate rather than cool or self possessed. She seemed scarcely to realise the dreadful circumstances of her position and she preserved all day the same apathetic air until her advocate began to plead on her behalf and then the tears occasionally trickled down her visage. The prisoner's physiognomy decidedly outlines low intellect and the likelihood that animal passion on being aroused might overbear her reason and hurry her on to deeds of violence; and this we think could easily have been predicated without any reference, the awful charge on which she was arraigned."

Other reports said that she "was very pale, but no other signs of agitation were visible on her face or in her manner. Crossing her hands in front (an attitude which she maintained almost through-out the whole of the trial) she looked hard, and as if with some curiosity, but with an expression of great coolness, at the Judge and the legal gentlemen within the bar. She is described as black-haired, and wearing a small straw bonnet with green trimming and two shabby gum flowers, and her shoulders covered with a grey woollen shawl. She was rather below the average stature and did not appear to be very strong. Her countenance was dull and heavy, and, without being repulsive, indicated a course animal nature. Thick and protruding lips almost disfigured the lower part of her face, the whole countenance being marked by the dull and vacant expression arising from a heavy languid eye and gaping mouth". There was a strong belief during the nineteenth century in the pseudo science of physiognomy which claimed that there was a strong relationship between a persons outward appearance and their inner character. Although it had its origins in ancient Greece the theories had gained particular popularity by the middle of Victoria's reign, illustrated by the descriptions of Mary in all the newspaper reports.

The day began in some confusion as when Lord Deas stated the charge to Mary she replied "guilty, my lord, yes I'm guilty". It was only after the question was explained to her by her counsel and she made a formal plea of not guilty that the trial began. The first witnesses called were William Dunbar followed by George Hamilton, who were asked to prove the three declarations Mary had made "freely and voluntarily while she was in her sound and sober senses and after she had been solemnly warned," and they also deponed, asserted under oath, that Mary's green tartan dress and blue petticoat were the articles referred to in the declarations.

Carte de Visite of Lord Deas by John Horsburgh of Edinburgh.

The small court room with its packed public gallery then saw the arrival of Agnes McLellan in the witness box. She confirmed that she had known the Hannahs "all my days" and also knew Francis Timney and his wife. She described Ann as a "very quiet, decent woman about 40 years old and she was stouter than me, rather a stout woman." She went on to say how Susan Timney had called to ask her to bake as her mother was poorly. Describing the house as a 'but and ben' she explained that after Ann's mother died she had been in the habit of going in to see her friend who she had found "lying on the kitchen floor in a pool of blood." She told the court that she had said "oh dear me Ann, what's ado" but there was no reply.[4] Hurrying to Knocknalling Lodge, the home of Mr and Mrs Coates, for help she also came across John McAdam, a servant of Mr Kennedy (the owner of Knocknalling) and they all ran back to Carsphad.

Agnes said: "Robert Coates turned her up to see if her throat was cut. It was not. We lifted her and put her in bed. The blood was all over the floor in different pools. Ann said twice 'oh dear.' That was all she said. She was on her face, her hands crossed below her head. Her cap was off. Her hair was all down and bloody. There was a knife – a butcher's knife – all bloody lying on the floor. There was also a poker with blood and hair on it, it was of the colour and appearance of Ann Hannah's hair. The blood on the floor was clotted and dried where it was thin. The flagged floor was broken and uneven and the blood had run into holes. There were sparks of blood on the legs of the table and on a chair. The furniture was not in disorder but standing in its proper place. There was a washing tub at the window and clothes, as if wrung, on the floor as if they had fallen from the table. The dish they had been in was upside down."

Asked to describe the house Agnes explained that kitchen door was to the left of the outer door, (which was divided in two) and the window looked out to the front. The fireplace was in the gable wall. Ann had been found lying with her head towards the window and her feet towards the fire, the iron poker at her right hand. On being shown the knife, Agnes said that when she'd seen it in the farmhouse it had been "all over with blood, blade and handle both." Agnes McLellan told the court that Mary had arrived about five minutes later and said "Dear me Nanny, the like o' this never was here before."

The next witness was Elizabeth McCormick or Coates who lived at Knocknalling Lodge, about a quarter of a mile from Carsphad. She said she had been alerted by Agnes McLellan and described how they had found Ann Hannah lying in a pool of blood, she 'didn't know if she was alive or dead." John McAdam, who in turn had been alerted by Elizabeth Coates, told the court he had assisted in putting Ann Hannah into her bed. When Mary Timney arrived he'd asked her if she'd seen no person on the road and when she'd said no, he'd said that it was strange such a thing could take place and her children going about and see nobody about the place. She'd answered that she'd been poorly and had not been at the door from the time her husband went away to work that morning. In his statement, Robert Coates, a woodsman from the Knocknalling Estate, repeated much of what had been stated by the previous witnesses.

Dr Andrew Jackson, a surgeon from Dalry, said he had arrived to find that it was clear Ann Hannah was dying. "She was alive and breathing. Her head was covered in blood and there was a considerable quantity of blood on the floor." Under cross examination he explained that the wounds, particularly on the right of her head, had, in his opinion, been done by a blunt instrument and they were "very serious, sufficient to account for the state she was in." He added that "the smaller fractures might have been inflicted by the poker, those on the face by the knife." On being shown the mallet, he said that this weapon could have inflicted the larger wounds, "any one of the wounds producing the fractures might have produced insensibility" he had no doubt that Ann Hannah had died of these wounds.

Dr Jackson confirmed that he had assisted doctors Shand and Millman with the post mortem and the resulting report to the Procurator Fiscal. "Death had been caused by the effect of extensive wounds of the head and face and compound fractures of the skull. The wounds were ten in number and varied from one inch to seven inches. On the left side there was a circular depression not more than a sixth of an inch in diameter but on the right side there were extensive fragments. Each forearm had six contusions. On examining the interior of the skull a fracture was found to traversects the base uniting the two points of fracture at each temple thus completely dividing the skull into two portions." The deceased had also suffered extensive bruising to the left temple, forehead, eyelids and nose and suffered two fractured ribs on the right. On being shown the weapons Dr Jackson confirmed that they could have caused the injuries. Under cross examination from Mr Cowan he stated that the wounds could not have been caused by a fall, even from a height onto a stone floor. "A person tripping and falling could not receive such wounds, though the person were large and heavy it would not effect the matter.

A violent push would not give the same effect as a fall from a height," he explained.

Dr John Shand, physician at Kirkcudbright, confirmed that the wounds were consistent with being caused by weapons shown to him in court and "could not have been self inflicted. Even if standing on a chair and pushed off, that would not have caused such wounds." In cross examination, Mary's counsel, raised the possibility of wounds being self inflicted by people who were discovered later to be ambidextrous, who had struck themselves with a poker and then fallen off a chair. "Suppose a person stood on a chair or table and struck himself on the back of the head and had fallen to the ground, could these injuries have been so inflicted?" Mr Cowan asked. "I think not. The points of fracture were too many to have been one fall," was the doctor's reply. Mr Cowan suggested that if there had been a struggle and several falls, could the falls have produced the wounds? Dr Shand admitted that this might have produced one of the severe wounds but a fall on the floor could not have produced the large wound on the right side of the head. Dr John Millman agreed with the evidence given by his fellow physicians but admitted that he had actually accidentally caused one of the wounds during the post mortem.

William Hannah, the next witness to be called, told the court that the farmhouse at Carsphad had two rooms, his sister slept in the kitchen and he shared the other with his brother. He described Ann as "a quiet woman, in good health who worked on the farm." He and his brother had left the farm before nine o'clock as they were working at Greenloop three miles away. The Timneys had taken over the tenancy of the small cottage when his mother had owned the farm. "Mrs Timney had been in the habit of borrowing things from my mother, she'd also borrowed tea and sugar from my sister, sending the children to borrow but she latterly refused to lend her anything," he said "I lent her husband, two shillings and sixpence that morning a little after seven o'clock as he said he was going from home all week and there was no money in the house.

They had also had words about carrying away wood from our farm about four or five weeks before. I had no difference with Mrs Timney about taking away wood but I told her I would not allow her to take it. My sister objected to her carrying away the wood. My sister told me of the difference. That was the second time my sister differed with her, it was in the same week, first was on Tuesday the other on Friday. I never knew them quarrelling before. I told my sister to evade having words with her as she told me the prisoner had been down with a stane in her hand to strike. I told her not to quarrel, we were to have quietness. I saw the prisoner that morning going to the pig house but had not spoke to her for a month, and I didn't then." Following the attack William Hannah said that he had searched the house and had found his own money but afterwards missed some tea and some sugar. He explained that the knife found on the kitchen floor had been bought for killing pigs and he'd told his sister not to use it in case she might spoil it, the last time he'd seen it it had been on a shelf at the back of the dresser. He said his sister had said nothing about washing that day as she'd washed at the end of the previous week.

Lockhart Paterson Hannah then took the stand and said that on the morning of the thirteenth he and William had left the farmhouse at about eight o'clock, Ann, who was a quiet woman of a cheerful disposition, had not quite finished her breakfast. He was in the habit of speaking to Mary Timney but hadn't that morning. He explained how, after getting the news about his sister, he had followed with the cart but was not within a mile of the house when he was met by his brother who wished him to go to New Galloway to fetch the constable. He had been at the Timney's house, he said, on the previous Saturday and Sunday nights when Mary asked him what he and his brother had been doing lately and Frank Timney had asked him what he was doing on Monday. Mary asked him if they were going to Greenloop on Monday and Lockhart replied if the weather was good. He confirmed that the prisoner had been wearing the green tartan dress that was now amongst the evidence.

The next witness to give evidence was the police constable for New Galloway, John Robson who said he had been told by his children that something had happened at Carsphad and not long afterwards he'd met Lockhart Hannah. He had arrived at the scene at about six o'clock and twenty minutes later he went to Francis Timney's cottage. "The house consists of one apartment with box beds which make a kind of partition. I found Mrs Timney in bed and four children, the eldest about ten years old and the youngest fourteen months. I got Mrs Timney to rise out of the bed. William Millman and James Haugh were with me. I said I wished to examine the clothes she was wearing and she gave me her polka jacket, flannel petticoat and a shift. I saw these articles were marked and stained, apparently with blood."

At this point there was an outburst from the prisoner who rose to "contradict one of the police officers in his too faithful description of the miserable dwelling in which she lived at Carsphad" one report claimed adding, "in doing which her eyes lighted up with a sudden fury, her voice shook, and her frame seemed to tremble with passion." Mary rose and said: "What lies you have been telling on me today. You told a lie just now when you said that my beds were closet beds when all the neighbours know they have curtains. You say that my things were marked with blood; shew me them."

Continuing, PC Robson said he had gone to the loft of the house by standing on top of a barrel, taking hold of the joists and pulling himself up. Here he had found a tartan dress, a bed gown, a petticoat and a child's night dress. The dress had been wet as if newly washed and there were several spots on other things, apparently blood; the bed gown, the petticoat, were marked with fresh blood. "It was distinctly wet with blood at the bottom when I first saw it. The sleeve of the shift was wet at the wrist. The colour was blood and I believed it was blood. The night dress was a little wet as if it had been washed." All the items had been bundled up in the tartan dress. On being shown the beetle, he answered: "I found that at the back of a barrel. It was very wet at the time as if it had been newly washed. I left it near where I found it as I did not think it was of importance."

Among other items found by the policeman were a handkerchief and seven farrells of oatcake in a chest, seven shillings and sevenpence in a glove on a dresser shelf and some tea and sugar mixed together in a cloth. He left the cottage after eight o'clock and went back after ten when he apprehended Mrs Timney and took her and her children away. On the fifteenth of January he returned to the cottage and his fellow officer Mr Richardson took possession of the beetle. "We noticed stains upon it at that time," he said.

The townspeople packed into the public gallery then watched as the first of the young girls was brought in to give evidence, an ordeal for anyone let alone children who had spent their lives in such a remote rural glen. Eleven year old Agnes Sproat, the daughter of John Sproat explained how she lived with her grandfather and passed both the cottages at Carsphad on her walk to school each day. On the morning of the thirteenth she'd seen Ann standing at her door and had asked the time. She'd told her she was in good time and had also given her a message for her grandfather. She confirmed that she'd seen the Timney children but not their mother. She was followed onto the witness stand by Jane Barbour, aged ten, who said she had gone into the Timney's cottage where Mrs Timney was drying something with a cloth. She confirmed that Mary had been wearing the tartan dress. Her seven year old sister Margaret was brought in next and she was examined without being sworn in, instead she was asked to state to the court that she had learned her catechism and knew that it was a sin to tell a lie. She was asked to identify the dress, which she did saying she had seen Mrs Timney in the tartan dress "with the red stripes."

It was then the turn of Mary's own daughter. The law had only recently been changed allowing a child to give evidence against a parent. Her appearance in the court produced an "evident emotion" from the public gallery which "rose to a painful height as her examination was proceeded with." Susan, who stated that she was under ten years old, was described as "an interesting looking little girl" by the press who added that she answered the questions with visible reluctance and not until they had been pressed on her repeatedly by the Advocate Depute and also by Lord Deas. It is, of course, now almost unimaginable that a child would be asked to give evidence in this way, let alone be bullied by the prosecuting advocate and the judge. Susan eventually admitted her mother had been wearing the tartan dress and that she had seen her go out to feed the pigs and she'd seen the girls on their way to school. Despite being pressed for an answer she twice denied seeing her mother go out again after this. Eventually Lord Deas said "You must tell us. We cannot let you away till you answer this question." Asked again if her mother had gone out, the child burst into tears.

In the end Susan replied that she did not recollect seeing her mother go anywhere that morning and continued to deny the questions. Asked if she remembered speaking to George Hamilton, [one of the legal team involved in the precognition] she confirmed that she did recollect him. She was then asked: "Did you not tell that gentleman that your mother had gone out to the Hannah's cottage after the children had passed to school." There was then a considerable hesitation until she finally answered yes. Asked if it was true what she had told the gentleman Mr Hamilton, she answered no. The Advocate Depute asked "did you say your mother came out of the Hannah's house and that there was something particular about her dress?" To which Susan answered no. Lord Deas then asked: "Did you say anything about her dress at all?" Susan again said no. Susan was finally removed from the court and her seven year old sister Margaret carried in but she was sent away again without being examined. Lord Deas addressed the jury saying that he though it right to state that the gentlemen who had previously examined the children were in attendance to give evidence as to what they said but he thought it better, under the circumstances of the case, not to bring them forward with the view of contradicting the statements of the last witness.

By this time it was half past three and the court briefly adjourned for the jury to have refreshments. The prisoner was also temporarily removed. As the court recommenced James Richardson, the police officer from Carsphairn was brought to the stand. He said that about a week before Ann Hannah's death he had been passing Mrs Timney's cottage and she had asked for a loan of sixpence as there was "neither money nor meat in the house" but he had refused. Mary Barbour also testified that on the previous Tuesday Mrs Timney had asked for a loan of 10d or a shilling but she had not given her it.

Agnes Corrie, a dairymaid from Knocknalling, then said that on the Friday before the prisoner, who was wearing the tartan dress, had arrived at the house asking for the housekeeper to see if she would give her a little tea. The witness had refused to fetch the housekeeper and the prisoner had gone away.

Dr Douglas Maclagan, the expert from Edinburgh had been asked to test a number of items taken from the Timneys, either on the evening of the murder or during the later searches.[5] He explained that after examination "microscopic and chemical" he found blood on the heavy part of the beetle and in one or two cracks in it. He reported that the stains on the bed ticks were old and those on the child's pinafore and the polka jacket appeared to be vegetable juice. There was no blood on the flannel petticoat and the blood on the shift was, he believed, menstrual. The green tartan dress had a brown stain on the right shoulder, the right elbow and at the wrist, the bed gown was similarly stained. He had used crystals of hematite to test for blood. Asked about the microscopical test Dr Maclagan explained that "if you get blood globules – corpuscles – you would find if they were not round that they were not those of a human being." He agreed that oval blood globules were those of a fish or bird. He also agreed under cross examination that the "blood corpuscles of the mammalia gave the same chemical reaction as the blood of any mammal." After further questioning he explained that the use of crystals of hematite was "very satisfactory when you get a satisfactory result but it is difficult to get this as I failed in finding it answer blood from my own arm." He agreed to a change in the wording of his report from human to mammal. Lord Deas clarified this: "You mean that it does not refer to human blood any more than any other mammal?" The doctor replied "yes." He went on to admit that he had concluded that the blood on the dress was not menstrual due to the position of the stains and the quantity. "If the dress had been worn and menstrual blood thrown upon it or the woman had lain on it these stains might have been made but from their quantity and size that was hardly conceivable," he said. The doctor explained that he had examined a specimen of Ann Hannah's hair and compared it under the microscope with hairs found adhering to the wooden beetle. "These were found to be fine human hairs and were quite the same tint and average size as the sample of Ann Hannah's hair. It is therefore the highest degree probable, though of course it cannot be absolutely affirmed, that these were from the same individual."

Sarah Glendenning or Smith, the wife of Dalry grocer, William Smith, said that no one from the Timney family had been in the shop. This was repeated by her husband, David Cowan, another shopkeeper from the village, and his assistant Robert McNaught, though Mr Cowan did say that someone had bought five and a half stone of meal for Mrs Timney during the previous week.

Samuel Good, married to Mary's mother Margaret Corson, stated that he was reeling yarn on the thirteenth and his wife had been "about the house all day." He added that his wife had not been to Carsphad since before harvest. Margaret Corson's presence at home in Dalry was confirmed by his daughter, Jane, and their neighbours Mrs Erskine Fisher, Jane Stevenson and Mary Douglas who all said they had seen her doing her washing that day.

No exculpatory evidence was produced. Mr Cowan, Mary's defence counsel then stood up to read the three declarations made by his client. Before 1898 an accused person was not a competent witness in their own trial and so were not supposed to speak. The only competent means of getting an accused's version of events into a trial was through prior statement before the sheriff, known as judicial examinations, though this statement was not on oath. Mary's first statement, given the day after Ann Hannah's death, read: "On the Wednesday before Christmas she went to gather some sticks that came down by the flood when Ann Hannah stopped her and said she was not to gather them and she called her a thief, stating that she had stolen her turnips. She denied it and words passed between them. She had not seen her until she went in with the neighbours on the day of her death. She said she had been unwell on the morning. She admitted the clothes were hers and said the tea and sugar had been bought by her daughter Susan in Dalry at William Smiths on Saturday night. She said that the blood was from her "courses" and she had not been wearing the clothes shown to her. She said she did not injure Ann Hannah and she was innocent."

On the seventeenth of January Mary was shown the wooden mallet that had been found at her cottage and she made a statement to say that she had never seen it before. On the third occasion Mary declared that her mother, Margaret Corson, had murdered Ann Hannah. "She said her mother came to the house to wash clothes for her. She was lying in bed with the infant, the other children were gathering sticks. Her mother changed into her clothes as she had her good ones on that she'd worn at the Sabbath. Mother said Mary I have a mind before I leave this world to give Ann Hannah her licks for setting your man against you when you were taken to Kirkcudbright. I replied that she wasn't to mind that as I never mind it now. I said Mother don't go for Ann Hannah is stronger than you and she'll fell you. But she went. Ten or twelve minutes later my mother returned all over with blood and I said preserve me mother, has Ann Hannah killed you? She said no Mary but I think I have near killed her. She took off my frock and petticoat and put on her own. She also took off her bedgown which I said was mine but now say is hers. She then washed her hands and face in my tub. She said, now Mary after what I have done to Ann Hannah I can neither stop to bake or wash nor rest and I must away home to be out of the road. I said Mother, put the kettle on and have a cup of tea before you go. She said no, she would be about at the Clachan by one o'clock. She left at a quarter or twenty to twelve and said I was not to tell that she had been to my house. I said Ann Hannah would say. She said she thought she'd given her more than she thought she'd get the better of but if she did get better she would be punished. She said her mother had said she'd had words with her husband on Saturday and barely spoke to him and he didn't know she was away from the house." These statements were all that Mary's defence put forward for her case.

The Advocate General then addressed the jury, his speech reported in full. "In a quiet district of a quiet country a deed had been perpetrated which had made their ears tingle. A quiet working woman, well on the morning of the thirteenth January 1862 engaged in her usual avocations, left well by her two brothers, seen well by the school girls who passed her door, was found by one o'clock, cruelly murdered, lying in pools of her own blood in the middle of her own kitchen. It was no single accidental blow that gave her her death wounds. Whoever did it had no intention to leave her alive at all. Wound after wound, blow after blow had been inflicted on that woman, dealt, as you have heard from medical testimony, with considerable violence, so that her skull was fractured in four places, two of her ribs broken and arms discoloured with the strokes. She was found senseless, speechless and almost so for the only exclamation that ever passed her lips was one of pain 'oh dear' and she died from the effects of the wounds that evening."

"He surely did not need to occupy their time with putting it to them whether they were not quite satisfied without another word, that murder had been committed on Ann Hannah. It was with surprise that he'd heard the prisoner's counsel ask questions of the witnesses that Ann Hannah might have committed suicide. They must be satisfied this was not possible. It was not one fracture but four distinct ones, every one of which would have produced insensibility, for when a person's skull is fractured they could not stand up to give another blow. No eye but that of the perpetrator and Ann Hannah herself saw the deed committed. The Omniscient eye above saw it – but no human eye. They had, therefore, to put together surrounding circumstances to endeavour to get at the truth as to who perpetrated the deed."

"These bloody clothes and beetle told a tale and the prisoner's story shewed that she had guilt to conceal. The taking of the money and tea might not have been an object of the murder and the idea of taking them might have occurred afterwards; but the prisoner had none of these immediately before, they were found in her house after Ann Hannah's murder. The prisoner herself put a motive into the mouth of her mother when she alleged she said she would learn her to put ill between the prisoner and her husband."

Mr Cowan then rose to address the jury, beginning by pointing out that from the moment Ann Hannah met her death there "had been cherished much prejudice against the prisoner." He earnestly asked the jury to "discard from their minds anything they had heard before coming into the box which was prejudice to the prisoner." He pointed out that the evidence was circumstantial and reminded the jury of innocence till proven guilty. With regard to the third declaration, he asked the jury to remember the circumstances Mary Timney was in at the time. "She had been in prison for more than a fortnight and been before the Sheriff more than once. She, who it would be seen, was not a strong minded woman, had been wrought to such a state of feeling and desperation amounting to weakness of the mind, that she did not know well what she was doing when she entered the third declaration." He reminded the jury that the "case was one shrouded in mystery."

He argued that he had not meant to suggest that Ann Hannah had committed suicide but it had been right, for the sake of the prisoner, to ask whether such a thing was not within the range of possibility. There were other ways by which it was possible that the deceased could have met her death other than by the hands of the prisoner at the bar, he suggested. Mr Cowan claimed that he had "endeavoured to show that even if the Advocate Depute was correct – the offence was not so grave as to call for a verdict of murder. No proof had been led to shew that the prisoner had cherished malice or hatred against the deceased. There had evidently been a severe struggle in that small room and the injuries the deceased had sustained might have been caused by her head coming into contact with a chair, a table, a stone floor or any object on it."

He concluded that if the jury was satisfied that the prisoner was present when the injuries were sustained then it was quite possible for them to return a verdict of culpable homicide. He argued that Mary's going down to the house after the deed was to show her innocence. Mr Cowan's defence of Mary may have had some influence upon the jury had it not been for the damning summing up that followed from Lord Deas. After a long day in court with very little rest or respite for anyone there, the judge began his summing up at ten minutes to seven in the evening. The newspaper reports said that he then talked for almost an hour.

He asked the jury to consider three things; firstly did Ann Hannah come by her death by a second party and not by herself, secondly was the prisoner the party who inflicted the violence and thirdly if so, what was the character of the act, was it justifiable and if not was it murder or culpable homicide? Lord Deas then proceeded to answer his own questions. He told the jury the first suggestion (that Ann Hannah had committed suicide) was too absurd to be dwelt upon. Although it was true that no human eye saw the attack this was very generally the case, especially in deliberate murder, "nobody went to commit a murder intending to be seen" he told them.

Lord Deas continued: "If acts and circumstances, sworn by different witnesses, were woven into a complete web or formed the links of a perfect chain supplied from different quarters, it was impossible to have better evidence. If they had no reasonable doubt then they must remember that that kind of evidence was competent and, was often, the most satisfactory of all. As reasonable men they must not exclude any reasonable evidence." He told the jury that "there was a very small motive on the part of the prisoner for the commission of the crime. If it was done for gain, the gain must have been very small though for murder there could never be an adequate reason." Lord Deas said there was "no trace of a motive on any one else's part and whoever did the act must have done it from very small and inadequate motives." He then alluded to the short period of time when the crime was committed and the near neighbourhood of the prisoner, giving her the opportunity for the attack, which he added, did not prove that she did it.

He then pointed out the remarkable coincidence of her husband having borrowed money that morning as they had no money in the house but seven shillings and seven pence being found after it, no tea and sugar in the house but some found later. He said that all the prisoner's denials had been contradicted. Lord Deas told the jury that they could ask themselves the question that if the prisoner knew Ann Hannah had been murdered that morning, if the person who committed the murder was dressed in her clothes and had gone from her home and if the blood was that of Ann Hannah then if they had that proved out of her own mouth they might consider whether it was she or her mother who committed the offence. There was sufficient evidence to shew that the crime could not have been committed by the mother. If the facts as sworn were true then he was bound to tell them that it was murder.

The jury retired at twenty minutes to eight but as the hour struck they returned to the court to announce that they had unanimously found the prisoner guilty of murder. A juror later revealed that they had all immediately agreed she was guilty. "The prisoner's face did not blench in the least degree, nor was her expression perceptibly altered," one paper commented, "The dread words which thrilled the hearts of the onlookers seemed to have little influence upon her whose destiny they determined but when his Lordship in pronouncing sentence addressed her she fairly broke down and urgently and pathetically prayed for mercy at his hands."

Lord Deas then proceeded to pass sentence in a way later reported, even by those reporters who had called Mary a "savage and implacable monster" as "in the most unfeeling terms, and in a manner which can be characterised as nothing else than brutal." As he began to address Mary Timney the gravity of what had taken place before her finally began to dawn on the young mother and she woke from her silent, perhaps uncomprehending observation of the proceedings.

"You were well acquainted with Ann Hannah," Lord Deas began, "She and her brothers were nearest neighbours and they had been kind to you and your husband on many occasions. On the very morning of her death one of the brothers lent your husband half a crown. It appears that you had taken offence at the deceased because she had declined to continue these loans and charitable donations that she had been in the habit of giving you. You seem also to have some cause of offence against her. She had accused you of taking wood and you say she accused you of stealing turnips. Whatever these causes were they were miserably small to have produced the result they seem to have produced. Even if there were more of them than we know of, it was impossible to suppose that they could be any other than the most miserably small causes to lead to such an act as that which you committed that day.

"Upon that day, Monday the thirteenth of January last, you went to her house at, it appears, somewhere about ten in the morning, carrying with you the mallet – that heavy deadly, instrument which we have exhibited here today and with which you must have inflicted repeated severe blows upon the head of that unfortunate woman till her skull was fractured in a manner which I do not remember of having ever before seen proved in a court of justice. With that mallet and iron poker which you found in the house of the deceased, you inflicted these injuries which left her there insensible and were more than enough to produce death, and in consequence of which, she died that same evening. In these circumstances, the jury, an intelligent and attentive jury, have after all the consideration they have given to your case, unanimously found you guilty of the crime of murder. It was impossible for anybody who heard the evidence to expect there should have been any other verdict."

At this point Mary, who had been sitting impassively through the long hours of the case, watching witness after witness speak against her with no one brought in her defence, cried out in tears: "My Lord it never was me, it never was me."

Lord Deas continued: "The time of all of us in this world is short, with most of us it is uncertain, but it is necessarily short in you case. Your days are numbered. They must indeed, be very few."

Mary again cried out: "No my Lord, no my Lord."

"I recommend you to use well those few days which you have yet to live," he went on. Again Mary cried out appealing to him to give her anything but that "let the Lord send for me" she begged.

Unmoved Lord Deas recommended that she use the short time she had left in the world making her peace with God adding "I should betray my duty and hold out false hope to you if I gave you the slightest hope that the sentence of the law might not literally be carried into effect."

As Mary continued to plead for imprisonment he put on the black cap and told her that she would be fed on bread and water until the twenty-ninth April and upon that day she would be taken to a place of execution and there by the hands of the common executioner to be hanged by the neck upon a gibbet until she was dead. "And may God have mercy on your soul" he said bringing the proceedings of the court to a close.

"The prisoner became more pale and excited," *The Kirkcudbright Advertiser* reported, "she said in the most heard rending tones 'oh my weans, my Lord dinna dae that, oh dinna dae that, oh my weans, oh my weans, dinna dae that." The unhappy prisoner, with her eyes turned beseechingly towards his Lordship, was taken from the bar crying 'my weans, my weans'. The scene was harrowing in the extreme and affected many to tears. Mary was led down the trap still crying 'my weans, my weans.' Thus terminated this solemn and painful trial at about a quarter to nine having lasted fully ten hours."

Seven

"When the black cap was assumed there was a thrill of horror ran through the court which had its effect on her for she cried and beseeched his Lordship to spare her life"

"No incident which has occurred in the Stewartry of Kirkcudbright for a great number of years has caused so much excitement and sensation as the trial of Mary Timney for the murder of Ann Hannah at Carsphad on the thirteenth January last," read *The Kircudbright Advertiser* editorial in the edition following the long day that ended with a sentence of death for the young woman.

Ever since "the deed was committed rumour has been busy circulating all kinds of stories in reference to the person charged with the crime but all was brought to light when the unfortunate woman stood her trial at Dumfries Circuit Court," the editorial continued. This statement was actually some way from the truth, and an examination of the witness statements in a later chapter will show how much information was not brought out in court. Whilst the newspapers had felt able to provide blow by blow accounts of what they imagined had happened in the attack they had not published the details of the rumours that had been rife around the region and two poems written about the case can only hint at what may have been on the lips of people in the Glenkens. The frenzy of speculation that preceded the trial was, however, replaced by the sober reality of the death sentence, a final punishment that few would have expected.

Although the "Bloody Code" had existed for many years there had been several attempts during the first part of the nineteenth century to bring changes to the law, with varying degrees of success. The news of the sentencing must have caused a feeling of despair, not just for Mary and her children but also in the heart of Dumfries Burgh's Member of Parliament, William Ewart, a man who had spent his life campaigning against the death sentence. Born in Liverpool in 1798, Ewart had been educated at Eton and Oxford and gone on to become an advanced liberal and social reformer, a Radical, who was a leading figure in the campaign for the end of capital punishment for many years. He first entered parliament in 1827 after a successful career as a barrister and only seven years later he helped to stop the practice of hanging criminals in chains. He was also instrumental in bringing about an end to the death penalty for minor offences like stealing cattle. From 1841 to 1868 he represented the Burgh of Dumfries and during that time, although he also became a vigorous campaigner for working class education and public libraries, he remained a passionate abolitionist.

Before 1834 there had been fifty crimes punishable by death in Scotland, (around three hundred in England) but there had been a series of changes restricting the number of capital offences and in 1887 the *Criminal Procedure (Scotland) Act* reduced the death penalty to cases of murder, attempted murder and treason. In 1840, the year before he became the honourable member for Dumfries, William Ewart led a group of abolitionists in parliament and managed to gain ninety votes in favour of the complete abolition of capital punishment. This proved to be a high point of the campaign as the support that had previously existed amongst the influential writers and essayists of the time, changed. Charles Dickens, for example, began to focus his criticism on the crowds who turned out to see public hangings rather than the executions themselves. It seemed that as the number of crimes punishable by death reduced so did the widespread support for the abolitionist cause. The death penalty, however, remained a public spectacle and as Mary counted the numbers of the days she had left, the councillors of Dumfries began to make preparations for her execution, but there was a great reluctance to carry out the task. The sentencing by Lord Deas had not only appalled many in the public gallery but it had been a sobering slap to the people who had followed the case with such prurient interest. There was a marked change in mood of the newspaper coverage following the trial.

An editorial in *The Kirkcudbright Advertiser* described Mary as "not at all repulsive, she is twenty-seven years of age and does not look more, of the average height, dark complexion and expression of countenance which does not indicate anything so bad as the commission of the crime for which she has been tried and condemned to death. When her children were brought into court as witnesses against her, a tear was observed in her eye and her cheek flushed when her eldest girl stated without hesitation that her grandmother was not at Carsphad on the day of the murder. The prisoner did not seem to comprehend the meaning of the words and was only awakened to a sense of her position when Lord Deas began his address before passing sentence. Then she seemed to know that all was over and when the black cap was assumed there was a thrill of horror ran through the court which had its effect on her for she cried and beseeched his Lordship to spare her life. Everything seemed to rush to her memory at once. She wished her own life spared at first and then remembered her children. The scene while she was being removed from the dock was painful in the extreme and affected many in court."

The editorial added that though there was much feeling for Mary's position, the evidence against her had been conclusive. "There was not a link in the whole chain which was not joined and considerable care must have been taken by the authorities in getting up the evidence." Special mention was then made of the New Galloway constable who had been "left for a day and a night to himself to do what he thought best in the course of justice and did not betray his trust. We hear that efforts will be made for a reprieve."

As the tide of feeling towards Mary turned following the trial, efforts were initiated for a commutation of the sentence. In 1862 there was no right of appeal in criminal cases in Scotland; the Court of Criminal Appeal would not be created until 1926. The normal procedure in the case of a person sentenced to death was a petition to the Queen.

Between 1800 and 1868 two hundred and seventy three people were publicly hanged in Scotland, fourteen of them women. A further two hundred and seven people had been sentenced to death but their sentences had been reprieved or respited. In 1860 all four murder convictions were reprieved including the case of Margaret Hannah, heard at the court in Stranraer, who had killed her illegitimate child. In 1861 three of the four people sentenced to death, including two women and a man accused of murdering his wife, had seen their cases commuted, so initially there was every reason to believe that Mary's fate could be changed.

Almost immediately after the trial a meeting was called at the Dumfries Council Chambers "for the purpose of adopting measures having for their object the commutation of the sentence of death passed upon Mary Reid or Timney." A large audience gathered and the meeting began with Dumfries grocer, Mr Johnstone, calling Dr James Murray McCulloch to the chair. Dr McCulloch, a well known medical doctor in the town, was also known as a Liberal politician, public speaker and supporter of the Temperance movement. He immediately informed the crowd that the gathering had been called "not through mawkish sentimentality, a feeling of philanthropy or soft heartedness." He emphasised the need for the case to be represented as it was. "Mary Timney was the person who murdered the other woman, that was perfectly clear and a more brutal, savage murder could scarcely be perpetrated." Though the meeting had been called in favour of a reprieve for Mary, Dr McCulloch's arguments would not be immediately recognisable as supportive to a modern audience. "If you read the account of every step of her unreasoning, stupid, senseless behaviour when about this murder and her insane attempt to implicate her own mother by concocting a story that a child of ten years of age would have more brains than to think would pass for fact," he said, "if they enquired into the private history of this woman and if they saw her sitting in the felon's dock with a face stolid, unmeaning, unintellectual, almost stupid, I think you would agree with me that if not an idiot she was the next step to it and morally and religiously speaking you might almost hold that she could not be held responsible for her actions."

The reporter covering the event for *The Kirkcudbright Advertiser* wrote that there was some applause at the end of this statement, though some disapprobation was also expressed. Dr McCulloch carried on pointing out that no woman had been hanged since Mrs Manning[1] (in 1849) and many females with crimes as bad as Mary Timney's had their sentences commuted to perpetual banishment. "The great majority of the public of Dumfries were horrified and indignant that such butchering should be permitted in their street," he added. Dr McCulloch expressed the widespread feeling amongst liberal abolitionists that public executions had a brutalising impact on the population. He said he was concerned about the effect "this spectacle of legalised strangulation of a human being and that of a wife and mother would have on the minds of those who witnessed it, especially on the minds of the young and rising generation."

The editor of *The Dumfries Standard*, Mr William McDowall, who would be a fervent supporter of the campaign, read the wording of the petition that would be sent to Her Majesty the Queen. "To Her Most Gracious Majesty, the Queen, the Petition of the undersigned inhabitants of the Royal Burgh of Dumfries and neighbourhood, humbly shewth that a young married woman, named Mary Reid or Timney, now lies in the prison of Dumfries under sentence of death for the murder of Ann Hannah at Carsphad in the Stewartry of Kirkcudbright, on the thirteenth of January last; and that this dread sentence will be carried into effect on the twenty-ninth of the current month, unless your Majesty should see fit in the exercise of the Royal prerogative to commute it into a milder punishment. "

Although the petitioners addressed their plea to the Queen, and firmly believed she would be involved in the decision making, in reality the responsibility had passed to the Home Secretary. Queen Victoria had been only nineteen years old when she'd ascended to the throne in 1837 and it had not been considered acceptable for her to preside over "hanging cabinets." The duty had therefore been delegated to the Home Secretary who administered the Royal Prerogative of Mercy. The trial judge would submit his report on each capital case and this was then considered by Home Department officials and made available to the Home Secretary. He was advised by his permanent officials but was also allowed to read the case papers for himself and have the final say. In some cases the trial jury would give a recommendation for mercy with their verdict and the presiding judge would pass this on with his own recommendations. The jury in Mary's trial had made no recommendation for mercy.

The petition put forward on Mary's behalf conceded that she had been fairly tried and convicted and did not dispute the legal justice of the sentence but they felt there were circumstances connected with the case which induced them to "cherish the hope that she is not placed outside the pale of mercy and that she is truly a fit object for the clemency and compassion of the Queen." At the meeting the Reverend Mr Ratcliffe from the Wesleyan church in Dumfries read out the grounds for the appeal. They were that "though not proven to be a lunatic or idiot, she must, from her appearance, and the stupid, irrational and absurd manner that she attempted to conceal the crime by putting it on her mother she might be considered as verging on idiocy and that for the other moral faculties and the blindness of her moral perceptions and the badness of her training she could not be held altogether responsible for her actions especially when excited by animal passions or propensities." They further argued that she was a woman and a mother and a great majority of the public in Dumfries and neighbourhood objected to the public execution.

The formal petition referred to Mary as "having laboured under the sad disadvantage of having been badly brought up. Ignorant in the extreme, without any moral training, of a very low type of character, extremely excitable and liable to be carried to the very verge of insanity." They claimed that she had committed the deed for which she had been condemned whilst in a "frenzied state to which she is constitutionally prone and specially caused by feelings of jealousy." The long and wordy petition which gave high flowing praise to Her Majesty concluded by pointing out that "rarely indeed, during the present century, has the capital punishment of a female taken place in Scotland and your Majesty's petitioners fondly trust that no such awful occurrence will be allowed to

PETITION TO THE QUEEN

IN BEHALF OF

MARY TIMNEY.

TO HER MOST GRACIOUS MAJESTY THE QUEEN, THE PETITION OF THE UNDER-SIGNED FEMALE INHABITANTS OF THE ROYAL BURGH OF DUMFRIES AND NEIGHBOURHOOD—

HUMBLY SHEWETH,

THAT a young married woman, named Mary Reid or Timney, now lies in the prison of Dumfries under sentence of death for the murder of Ann Hannah at Carsphad, in the Stewartry of Kirkcudbright, on the 13th of January last ; and that this dread sentence will be carried into effect on the 29th of the current Month, unless your Majesty should see fit, in the exercise of the Royal prerogative, to commute it into a milder punishment.

Your Petitioners humbly but earnestly beseech your Majesty to consider the case of this unhappy convict ; and by the exercise of the Royal prerogative to save her from a premature and violent death. They make this prayer on her behalf, on the broad grounds of sympathy with her, in her low and miserable estate ; and specially because they believe that, however much she may be stained with guilt, she is so exceedingly weak in intellect, so deficient in moral sense, and so deplorably untrained and ignorant, as to merit commiseration as well as punishment ; and that a penalty less than that of death might be graciously deemed by your Majesty to fully meet the requirements of the case.

Your Majesty's Petitioners believe that, assuming her to have been justly convicted, she must have perpetrated the fatal deed when wrought up to a pitch of frenzy by jealousy or other strong passion—a state of mind to which the unfortunate woman appears to be constitutionally prone. Your Majesty's Petitioners respectfully submit that the evidence tends to show that the blows which caused the death of the deceased resulted from a protracted affray ; the blood found on various parts of the prisoner's garments, and on the furniture of the apartment in which the deed was committed, all tending to substantiate this idea.

Your Majesty's Petitioners, on grounds such as these, venture to express a hope that your Majesty will lend an attentive ear to this humble Petition ; and they plead all the more earnestly for a commutation of the convict's sentence, because they consider public executions to be demoralising in their character, and that the spectacle of this poor young woman, who is also a wife and a mother, so put to death, would be inexpressibly revolting, and exercise on the community at large a brutalising influence.

May it therefore please your Majesty to consider this humble Petition, and to commute the sentence of death passed upon Mary Timney, in such a manner as to your Majesty may seem fit ; and your Majesty's Petitioners, as in duty bound, will ever pray.

A copy of the plea to Queen Victoria made by the Dumfries petitioners.

take place in Dumfries, where there has been no execution of any kind during the last thirty-six years."

There was general agreement amongst the speakers, including another minister, the Rev Mr Scott, that if all this information had been brought before the jury by her advocate, there may have been, if not another verdict, then at least a recommendation to mercy. Not everyone agreed with Dr McCulloch's observations of Mary though, others commented that they had been "astonished at the prisoner's self possession and mental control in the court." Dr McCulloch then revealed to the meeting that he had gone over the papers with the defence advocate on the night before the trial and had planned to object to some of the 'scientific evidence' as he regarded it as "no evidence at all." In the morning the Procurator Fiscal for Kirkcudbright, Mr Gordon had asked him why he was planning to appear. Dr McCulloch had then received a note to say that he would not be called as a witness as Dr Mclaggan had admitted some of the discrepancies in the evidence. According to the Dumfries doctor the Edinburgh man had admitted that it could not be proven that it was human blood and even if it could, that it could not be proven to have come from the victim.

Clearly impassioned by the injustice of the sentence, Dr McCulloch roused the meeting by saying "We all know that hanging by the neck until you are dead, dead, dead is the sentence in the case of murder; but many of us believe and many of us are mentally convinced of the impropriety, brutality and barbarism of such a punishment at all (there was applause the reporter noted) and in the second place we hold that in such a case as this of a woman whose mental capacity is so low, whose stupidity as proved by the stolid, unmeaning, brutish gaze with which she sat in the dock as fact after fact came out diminishing the days of her existence, these all proved clearly to me that I don't believe she is morally and religiously speaking, responsible for her actions. I believe that she is a human animal whose lower propensities – which we share with the animals – are invariably stronger than her will or moral powers and have obtained command over her and that as such she requires to be locked up as an irrational being ought to be."

In a further revelation about the case, a Mr F Nicholson told the meeting that he had spoken to one of the jurymen who told him that they had immediately come to a unanimous decision and what had taken twenty minutes was a discussion between them trying to find some mitigating circumstance on which to recommend mercy.

The women of Dumfries were also active in support of the campaign; on the Saturday following the trial a meeting of ladies had taken place at the school room at Loreburn Street United Presbyterian church. The meeting had been called by Agnes McCulloch, wife of Dr McCulloch, who along with her daughter Mary, believed that the women of the town should take action in sympathy with the prisoner. Chaired by the Rev Scott, the more than forty women present agreed to divide up to gather supporters from the town's districts for a petition that would be exclusively from women who wished a commutation of the sentence. Their petition suggested that the fatal occurrence might have happened in "an affray between the two women. The evidence tends to shew that the blows which caused the death of the deceased resulted from a protracted affray – the blood found on various parts of the prisoner's garment and the furniture of the apartment in which the deed was committed all tending to substantiate this idea."

The campaign received support from perhaps the most unexpected person – the victim's brother. After the publication of reports on the public meetings *The Dumfries Standard* and *The Courier* both received a letter written by William Hannah, of Carsphad, Kells. He wrote: "I wish to let Dr McCulloch and Mr McDowall know that I have no objection to that petition but I have objections to statements of theirs proposed to be inserted in that petition. I would wish to know how Dr McCulloch and Mr McDowall arrived at a motive for Mary Reid committing murder. They say it was specially caused by jealousy. Lord Deas could not arrive at that motive, her own counsel could not arrive at that motive or I doubt not they would. If Mary Reid has given a motive it was clearly proved that she could not be believed. Dr McCulloch also says that she is verging on insanity. I can tell Dr McCulloch that there was, I think, one very trivial incorrect statement in all the evidence brought against her which she quickly corrected, which I think should go far to prove that she was awake to what was going on. Neither is she so desperately ignorant as represented by Mr McDowall as Dr Maitland has baptised all her children on her own responsibility. Neither was she so miserably poor as mentioned, for her husband was getting thirteen shillings per week for his work. Therefore if there be a petition got up for to spare her life, as I hope there will, it must be a petition on some grounds other than these or they cannot be just grounds to present a petition on. But for humanity's sake I should like an attempt to be made."

The editor of *The Dumfries Standard* commented that the hope expressed in his closing comments did William Hannah "infinite credit" but he said that it was clear that Mary had been "reduced to great straits, although possibly by her own improvidence." He added that "as to the extreme ignorance of the prisoner in religious matters especially, there cannot be the shadow of doubt. The chaplain of the prison had in dealing with her to begin just as if she had been a heathen and had lived all her life hitherto ignorant of the very ABC of the Gospel."

But not everyone supported the campaign. The two main Dumfries newspapers, *The Standard* and *The Courier* had long been associated with rival political positions, the former siding with the Whigs or Liberals whilst the latter was closely aligned with the Tories or Conservatives. It was not surprising, given the stance of *The Standard* editor, that the Courier would come out with an opposing view. The two camps sat on either side of the argument that had raged throughout the century on the subject of capital punishment. *The Standard* was clearly against it and had been supportive of William Ewart's many attempts to abolish the penalty; *The Courier* was just as stubbornly in favour of it. Citing "God's own revealed warrant and command" the editor wrote that there were many thoughtful citizens who were not prepared for the abolition of capital punishment and could not plead for mercy in a "case of murder so aggravated."

The Courier editor was particularly indignant that the petitioners had included the "plea of jealousy" without expressing that the jealousy was, he felt, unfounded and therefore a "cruel insinuation, making the innocent murdered woman, doubly a victim." He referred to William Hannah's letter as proof that the farmer's sister was a "woman of spotless virtue." *The Courier* had little time for Mary's denial that the beetle was hers; the paper was firmly behind the view of Lord Deas that she had gone to Ann Hannah's house armed with it. "She denies that it was hers. How then did it come to be found in her own house after the murder? It must have belonged either to the Hannahs or the Timneys. If to the former, would the prisoner have taken it to her own house, where the finding of it could scarcely fail to connect her with the scene of violence? On the other hand, if the beetle belonged to Timney, she would not leave it in Hannah's house to be a proof against herself that she had been there with it, but would do precisely what she did, namely, take it away with her. This is more than a presumption that her denial of the beetle being hers is a falsehood; and this specific falsehood throws discredit at once on the whole of this fourth declaration of hers. But Mr William Hannah can tell that the beetle did not belong to his house."

The views of *The Courier* were echoed in reports and editorials published in *The Glasgow Herald*, a newspaper that would later in the year again side with Lord Deas with regard to another death sentence imposed on a woman. William McDowall, the Standard editor vigorously rebuffed their arguments against Mary. "He [the editor of *The Glasgow Herald*] falls into the egregious error of supposing that, as regards responsibility, all human beings (who are not positively insane) stand on an equal footing. If his words used on this subject have any meaning at all, it is that low organisation, want of education, heathenish ignorance and extreme destitution are not to be considered in such a case as this; but that Mrs Timney with her one or two talents is to be judged rigorously and dealt with as exactingly as if she had been rich in intellectual endowments and in worldly wealth, had been religiously trained, and hedged round by a host of favourable circumstances."

The Dumfries Herald and Register, however, also had little sympathy for the petitioners. "We think it highly probable that the grounds of being a woman will influence the Government to save the wretched woman's life. To do so would be in accordance with recent precedence for the capital sentence was not carried out a few years ago in the case of a most atrocious murder committed in London by a woman whose sex formed her only claim to life. The woman who commits a brutal murder on a person of her own sex by that act places herself beyond the pale of the privileges which man accords to the weaker vessel and enters the class who are the natural enemies of society and against whom society must take the most effectual measures of defence. It is sickening to think that within the space of a fortnight Mary Timney may be hanging betwixt the earth and sky, dying the death of a felon; but we must not forget that cottage kitchen in the Glenkens and the woman busy over her household work, struck down without warning by a cruel blow, her skull battered to pieces by repeated strokes and her blood poured out in pools on her own floor. The danger is that should the sentence of the law not be carried out the Carsphad Murder may be followed by other murders; that women may not only give free vent to their own hate but become instruments of man's rancour or greed, confident in their immunity from the punishment of death. It is for Sir George Grey to decide whether this risk may be run in order to avoid the painful proceeding of executing a woman."

Eight

"The principal motive was jealousy"

News of the campaign was kept from Mary, now on her diet of bread and water in Dumfries prison, for fear of giving her false hope. Although described in such critical terms even by her own supporters, information began to filter out that finally gave a more realistic picture of the young woman who had been so demonised in the weeks before the trial. Unfortunately for Dr McCulloch his theories about Mary, based on her appearance in court, were soon shown to be mistaken. She was visited by Dr W A F Browne, one of Her Majesty's Commissioners in Lunacy, in order to assess her state of mind. He came to the conclusion that she was "neither fatuous or an imbecile but possessed fully the intellect of her class but in answer to questions was almost entirely want of early moral training and education while, according to her account, her life had been passed under circumstances very unfavourable to moral development."

For the first few days following the trial Mary was in great mental distress, "her demeanour showing that she was fully alive to the dreadful fate that awaited her should the mercy of the Crown not be interposed to save her life from the scaffold." She wept bitterly, "completely prostrated by the doom" that had overtaken her. Under the ministrations of the prison chaplain Rev Mr Cowans, Mary became more calm and was able to "conduct herself with a wonderful composure." As time passed, the twice daily visits from the minister brought about a profound effect enabling Mary to sleep well and eat her food with, what was described as, 'an ordinary appetite.' Although she was living on bread and water, given the poverty of her life previously, her new diet was no worse and may have been somewhat better than she had been used to. Certainly the regularity of her meals must have been something of a change.

Public opinion continued to shift as details of her life became known. "Though there can be no doubt as to the low state of moral feeling to which the condemned prisoner has been brought in the course of a vicious career and perhaps by the force of bad example and training, she is far from being the ignorant being which from her appearance and circumstances she had been assumed to be. She is able to read and write and, being married to a Catholic, it has been her duty to stand sponsor for all her children at baptism – which in itself implies a certain amount of moral culture," *The Standard* reported.

Mary, at last, made a full confession to the minister. Whether it was due to her finally comprehending the gravity of her situation, a result of the minister's regular visits or perhaps simply because it was the first time since her arrest that someone had been able to advise her and was willing to listen, it is impossible to know. Her understandable ignorance of the legal system meant that she probably believed that there was a chance her admission would change her fate. Whatever the reason, she gave her account of what had happened on that Monday morning to the chaplain. The local newspapers reported that her "principal motive was jealousy" as she believed Ann Hannah had "acquired a great influence over her husband."

"On the morning she had left her own house with a rope to gather some sticks when she was accosted by the deceased who asked if she was going to 'thieve' more of their wood; that some high words and some blows ensued; that she returned to her house but later went to Ann Hannah's house to give her a beating but with no intention to kill her; on entering the kitchen she was met by Ann Hannah who gave her a violent kick with her clog above the knee inflicting a severe wound, the scar of which she still shows; that a fight was renewed blows being struck on either side and that in the course of this she seized a wooden mallet or beetle with which Ann Hannah had first struck her but which had fallen to the ground and with this weapon struck the deceased a blow on the side of the head by which she was stunned and in the heat of passion she had followed up this blow with others. She still denies that the beetle was hers."

The Glasgow Daily Herald's report of Mary's statement added that the wound she received was more than two inches in length and that it was whilst she was stooping that Ann Hannah had struck her flat on the back with the beetle which she had in her hand and which then dropped to the floor.

The statement was taken down and communicated to the Sheriff who then forwarded it to the Lord Advocate who in turn laid it before the Home Secretary, Sir George Grey. It was reported that although Mary had gained some composure after this she was still "much depressed in her spirits" and had been visited by her husband and children. The scene at parting was said to have been deeply affecting, "the prisoner appeared to be suffering the deepest anguish, taking leave of her children with tenderness and affection that could not have been expected in one whose past life is supposed to have done so much to blunt every moral feeling."

The Courier remained unconvinced by Mary's confession and raised questions, arguing that a woman, clearly the weaker of the two, would not have gone to her neighbour's house to "give her a beating" without some sort of weapon. "Nay, more as Ann Hannah is said to have been the first aggressor in the house, in giving Mary Timney a violent kick, she must have been prepared for the encounter; and yet being by far the stronger of the two, and having command of poker, knife, and beetle, all in her own house, she came to the most violent end in a struggle for life, without having been able to inflict the slightest scratch on the prisoner Timney – always excepting that alleged wound by the first kick. Now then, does man or woman in Dumfries really believe this story? Whosoever founds upon it, does farther wrong to the memory of that poor murdered woman."

Mary persisted in declaring herself innocent of any intention to murder, firmly adhering to her account of the incident that had resulted in Ann Hannah's death. During the twice daily visits from the chaplain she began to talk about the difficulties of her home life, though the newspapers shied away from reporting these details they did write that everyone who came into contact with her testified to "the low state of moral and religious feeling" and her "comparative ignorance of the great truths of Christianity which her conversation displayed."

As the days counted down, support for the petitioners gained momentum, the people of Dumfries rallying to the cause of getting Mary's sentence commuted. Whether it was out of sympathy for the young woman or because of a horror at the thought of a mother of four being hanged in their town, they signed the petitions in their thousands. By the twenty-fifth of April, two thousand, one hundred and seven signatures had been gathered amongst the men of the town and significantly, more than three thousand from the women, together almost half the population of Dumfries at the time. Petitions had also gained support in Thornhill, Annan, Kirkcudbright, Castle Douglas and even New Galloway. The campaign had been joined by the considerable political weight of Sir William Dunbar, the Member of Parliament for Wigtownshire who was also a Lord of the Treasury, James Mackie MP for the Stewartry, Mr Millar, MP for Leith and the Duke of Argyll. From the way the newspapers had portrayed Mary before the trial, the violence of her crime and given that she had tried to blame her own mother, it says a great deal about the community that significant numbers of people from this rural, sparsely populated region had some compassion for her once the details of her life began to emerge.

The petitions were at first sent to the MP William Ewart who had, not unexpectedly, taken a close interest in the case and was being updated daily on how things were progressing. He took them, in person, to the Home Department as it was then called and met with the Under Secretary, Mr Waddington as Sir George Grey had returned home to Hawick for Easter. The Lord Justice Clerk, the second most senior judge in Scotland and the Lord Advocate, the chief legal officer, had been written to and Mr Ewart was confident the latter would "open every avenue of defence for the prisoner." With his legal background, Mr Ewart was concerned that Mary had not been given a fair trial and on one matter in particular, he felt the judge had mislead the jury. In the April twenty-third edition, with just six days to go before the execution, Mr Ewart wrote to *The Dumfries Standard*: "I think the judge states in his summing up that the convict took the mallet with her from her cottage to commit the crime; hence he naturally infers malice prepense. But I also think it will be found that there is no proof of her having so taken the mallet." Other correspondents had also written to the paper about the same issue having drawn the same conclusions.

The editor commented: "All who are in circumstance to examine the matter know that this vital defect in the printed evidence is indisputable. The Home Secretary has been acquainted and has, we have reason to believe, called the attention of some of the leading law authorities in Edinburgh to this and other points. Should the defect be established, by reference to the judge's notes, it may be possible with the extenuating circumstances pleaded by the petitioners, to secure a commutation of the sentence. The Duke of Argyll's interest has been solicited on behalf of the convict, everything possible has been done to secure a mitigation of the sentence."

Aware that Sir George Grey had returned home to his estate for Easter, two of the leading campaigners, Agnes McCullough and her daughter Mary set off on the morning of Monday the twenty-first with the intention of lobbying the Home Secretary. They travelled by train to Newcastle and then went north on the Berwick line arriving at the private station of Sir George's estate at Fallodon near Alnwick just before nine o'clock at night. Despite the late hour Sir George "at once accorded them with an interview" receiving them with "great courtesy and consideration and entered minutely into the object of the mission, shewing in the course of the ensuing conversation that he was well conversant with the facts of the case and was all ready to a great extent familiar with the points on which the petitioners found their pleas for the commutation of the sentence" *The Standard* reported. He went on to repeatedly express his interest in the cause of the deputation and his resolution to do what he could "compatible with his sense of duty and regard for law and justice. " He told the ladies that he could not be more explicit and the issue could not be decided until he had "received answers to his inquiries on the subject from various quarters." After the half hour interview Mrs McCullough and her daughter thanked Sir George before catching the express, which had stopped for them at Fallodon, back to Newcastle where they stayed before returning to Dumfries the following morning. *The Standard* praised the deputation for travelling so far, "the distance to Fallodon being not less than one hundred and forty three miles," in order to add emphasis to the "written pleadings."

Whilst the most strenuous exertions were being made in an effort to get the sentence changed, preparations continued for the execution due to be held on Tuesday twenty-ninth of April, with the gallows following the same journey taken by the man who had condemned Mary to death. It had been so long since the last execution in Dumfries that the town's gallows had become outdated; "the instrumentality has been improved" one newspaper stated and the Town Clerk had been forced to apply to borrow one from Edinburgh. The deadly contraption was transported by train from Edinburgh arriving at Dumfries station on Thursday evening. The site chosen for the execution was the corner of Buccleuch Street and St David's Street, now known as Irish Street and work began the following day making the underplatform on which the gallows would rest. Mary was moved to a cell at the opposite end of the prison so she would not hear the "dreadful sounds of preparation."

On the morning of Friday the twenty-fourth of April, letters arrived for several people involved in the Mary Timney case, all of them bringing the same dreadful and disappointing news. Mrs McCulloch received two letters at her Castle Street home, only a short walk from the prison, one from the Home Department and a second from Sir George Grey personally, which detailed the considerations which had influenced him in his decision. It was not the news the petitioners had hoped and prayed for. William Martin, the Town Clerk was informed that he should press ahead with the arrangements. At the same time Mr Ewart, and other MPs involved in the campaign, also received letters from the same office informing him that "after the most careful consideration of all the facts of the case and after communication with the judge who presided at the trial, Sir George Grey regrets that he cannot see any ground which would justify him in recommending that the prerogative of the Crown should be interposed for the remission of the capital punishment."

Mr Ewart communicated his feelings to *The Dumfries Standard*, the newspaper that had fervently backed the petitioners: "It appears to me that they might have inferred the possibility of a fatal issue arising (in the beginning) from no premeditated intent to kill. But alas! The result is otherwise. I have used every effort on the side of Christian mercy. The rest we must submit to Heaven." In one final push, he made a personal appeal to the Home Secretary on the day before the execution. He wrote to the Standard's editor: "I am afraid that before this letter reaches you all will be over. As a final attempt I have just been reviewing the case with Sir George Grey and bringing again before him the main points on our side. But he has made up his mind. I should have been glad to telegraph you with an opposite consideration. But alas! There is no chance."

The officials at the prison had done their best to prevent Mary from knowing of the efforts being made to have her sentence changed but she had believed that her confession to killing Ann Hannah in a quarrel with no intent to commit murder might have exercised an influence on the sentence. *The Courier* reported that "ever since the date of her so called confession the unfortunate woman appears to have entertained the conviction that some effort would be made to save her life from the scaffold, and more than once she expressed her belief that she would not die that shameful death." When the information was received from the Home Department that there was no change in Sir George Grey's attitude, it was the responsibility of the prison governor Mr Stewart to break the news to Mary. The chaplain, Mr Cowans urged her to give up hope and she was overcome, shaking in terror and overwhelmed by grief. *The Belfast News Letter* reported that "she was seized with a nervous trembling from head to foot which increased to a convulsive fit. Her mental agony finding expression in almost inarticulate cries for mercy." "Day by day her bodily frame became weaker and it looked, at times, as if the powers of nature would give way before the executioner arrived to do his hateful work," *The Dumfries Standard* reported. "Throughout the night of the Saturday and Sabbath she slept little so great was the agony she endured and so shattered was her whole nervous system; and so confused had she become that she rose unusually early on Monday morning in the belief that her last hour was to hand. Her mental anguish was, there is reason to fear, caused as much if not more by the dread of an approaching painful death on the scaffold, as by a sincere heartfelt remorse or a lively contrition on account of her awful crime. Even in her most penitential moods, she never once varied from the statement in her confession as to the circumstances in which the murder was committed and it will be seen that in her last words on the subject – her dying declaration as they may be called – she adhered to the allegation that she had quarrelled with Ann Hannah but did not take her life."

After the trial Mary had been permitted to received three visits from her husband. Information leaked out to the newspapers that there was no affection expressed between them. *The Belfast News Letter* said: "On none of these occasions did either of them, though to some degree affected, display poignant grief, the dissimilarity of their ages, the poverty, jealousy and domestic strife in which they had lived having seemingly blunted the feelings of mutual affection." Her mother and

Whitehall
24 April 1862

Sir,

I am directed by Secretary
Sir George Grey to acquaint
you in reply to your application
on behalf of Mary Reid or Timney
now under sentence of death
for murder, that after the most
careful consideration of all
the facts of the case, and after
communication with the judge
who presided at the trial, Sir
George Grey regrets that he
cannot

James Mackie Esq MP
Castle Douglas N B

cannot see any ground
which would justify him in
recommending that the Prerogative
of the Crown should be interposed
by the remission of the capital
punishment.

I am, Sir,
Your obedient servant,
H. Waddington

A copy of the letter from the Home Department giving Sir George Grey's
decision not to grant a reprieve. This letter was sent to James Mackie, the
MP for Castle Douglas.

sister were allowed to see her and on the same day Frank visited with all the children except for the baby. The heart rending parting from her children belied all those press reports that had represented her as a 'savage and implacable monster.' Witnesses said that she had to be forcibly parted from her daughters, particularly the one she called her "sweet wee Maggie." She had little to say to her husband but as they left she asked him to "remember the weans and see that they are brought up well." Even *The Glasgow Daily Herald*, a paper with no sympathy towards the prisoner or her plight, admitted that they had been told that "of her children she spoke very frequently and in a very touching manner."

As she tried to put her life in order, Mary dictated letters firstly to her mother and sister and then to Mrs McCulloch and her daughter, who had campaigned so vigorously on her behalf. In the letter to the McCullochs she thanked the ladies for their great kindness in striving to get her life spared "a little longer" and to her poor dear children. She added again that she had not intended to kill Ann Hannah saying "this is the truth I speak." In a post script she gave her sincere thanks to the public of Dumfries for the great interest they had taken on her behalf. It was reported that after dictating the letters, which were "tolerably well written for a woman of her rank" she said that she wished to copy them out in her own hand. She began writing 'Dumfries Prison twenty-eighth April 1862. To Mrs and Miss McCulloch, Castle Street. Dear Ladies, I feel more thankful than I am able to say for the very great kindness you have shewn me in striving to get my life spared a little.'.. but at this point she saw the next phrase relating to her children and she broke down and fainted. On Monday evening as the chaplain prayed with her, Mary fell into an hysterical fit which lasted for several hours. The prison's medical officer, Dr Scott, was called for and he stayed with her for some considerable time before finally administering a dose of laudanum. She was put to bed and, by all accounts, slept well watched over in the cell by two female attendants. *The Glasgow Daily Herald* later reported that Dr Scott was of the opinion that "had her imprisonment been of much longer endurance she could not have survived till the morning of her execution."

The governor of the prison, Mr Stewart and his wife reported that Mary had repeatedly expressed her grateful thanks for their humane attitude towards her and evidently all the staff involved in her supervision and care expressed that she had been the object of extreme pity and solicitude. According to *The Dumfries Herald and Register* the daily visits of the chaplain had brought Mary some peace, "it is gratifying to know that her mind has been brought to such a state that she has been able to express a hope that through the merits of the Redeemer she may find peace with God." *The Standard* reported that "however it may be accounted for, we simply state the fact substantiated by prison officials, that the woman who was depicted on the day of the trial as a savage and implacable monster without a single redeeming feature in her character or her crime, exhibited during the latter days when not visited by the thoughts of her approaching doom, a subduedness of disposition allied to that of those in country districts who are called 'innocents' because they are harmlessly idiotical."

This photograph from 1900 shows the prison, a large plain fronted building on the right in the distance. The building was later demolished.

77

Nine

"She screamed aloud in tones that brought a shudder to the hearts of those who heard her 'oh no, oh no, oh my four weans, oh my four weans!'"

Even though the prison staff did their best to protect Mary from the preparations for her execution, the people of Dumfries were only too aware that the gruesome spectacle was going ahead. On the Monday evening workmen began to erect barriers at all the approaches to the prison. The burgh council had also sincerely hoped that Mary's sentence would be changed, perhaps on an humanitarian level but certainly in terms of the shame, disruption and cost to the town. In purely practical terms it was an event fraught with difficulties and dangers.

Although few death sentences were carried out, the majority being commuted to imprisonment, and fewer still held in Scotland, the burgh council was, nevertheless, aware that in some cases executions attracted large unruly crowds. They were fearful that, given the widespread objection to the hanging of a woman on top of the sea of change in the public's opinion on the case, there could be serious unrest. On the nineteenth of April William Martin, the Town Clerk, wrote to Sir George Grey asking for permission to second police officers from neighbouring forces and create special constables for the day. "The Magistrates do not anticipate anything like a riot on the occasion of the execution if it unfortunately should take place," he wrote, "but they think it right that every precaution should be taken that the disagreeable and painful duty should be done in decency and order." He argued that the number of constables available from the Dumfries force was "totally inadequate to preserve order" and the special constables could "not be relied upon" due to both a "feeling against capital punishment and a great repugnance to be engaged in any way with the execution of a woman."

Metropolitan hangings had, in the past, attracted huge crowds. The execution of the Mannings in London in 1849, referred to by Dr McCulloch at the public meeting, had been witnessed by 30,000 people[1]. In England, the vast majority of executions took place in assize towns during the early 19th century and were a key event in the county calender but in many rural counties, as was the case in Dumfries, the occurrence was so rare that sheriffs pleaded against death sentences fearful of the stain on the county's reputation. By the middle of the century the growing sensibilities of the Victorian middle classes had much to fear from the crowds drawn to these scaffold spectacles. Charles Dickens, at one stage a supporter of the abolitionists, had begun to recommend the ending of public execution not because of any liberal stand on capital punishment but in order to prevent the crowds 'enjoying' the event. After one such occasion in 1840 he wrote, "No sorrow, no salutary terror, no abhorrence, no seriousness; nothing but ribaldry, debauchery, levity, drunkenness and flaunting vice in fifty other shapes." [2]. There was a risk of crime such as pickpocketing, begging and damage to property being committed and there was also a risk of danger to life with so many people crowding into the streets around the prison. In the past spectators had been killed by crushing and panic, in 1807 twenty seven people died with a further seventy needing treatment at one execution at Newgate Gaol in London.[3]

It had been so long since the previous hanging in Dumfries that the authorities had little idea what to expect. Local people had become more sympathetic to Mary's plight but the case had been reported throughout Britain and there was no way of knowing how many would turn up in the town or what their motives might be. The erection of the barriers was one attempt to control the numbers immediately in front of the prison and the gallows. At the east end of Buccleuch Street, between the English Chapel and W McGowan's house opposite, a strong barrier was built, seven feet high made of "flooring laid edgeways between two stout joists fixed deeply in the ground." In the centre they placed a T gate so that any crush or surge in the crowd in Castle Street would have no effect on those in Buccleuch Street. From "Mr McKay's ironmongery warehouse" to across the street, stretched one barrier whilst another was built to protect the new United Presbyterian church "from intrusion." Another was built across St David's Street from the south corner of the store to the prison lodge and there was fencing of a small space so the police constables could walk as far as the corner of the "yellow house" and then further barriers across St David's Street at the Friar's Vennel, across Buccleuch Street from the prison door, and across the same street from the lower corner of the prison. Wickets were placed in all the fences which were guarded by police officers on the day to ensure that there was no crushing or "tumult." The public would be allowed through the fences at Castle Street, the Vennel and at the corner of the prison but none were to allowed within the inner space that would be occupied by the constables, police and Militia only.

The town's newspapers reported that "groups lingered about the north east corner of the jail yard all day – moving here and there – as if trying to find out where would be the best place to get a good view of the execution and in the evening crowds were continually passing out and in the barriers. The town had a busy aspect and strangers, but for the serious aspect of the people, might have thought it was the eve of some joyous holiday instead of that of a day of doom. There was a continual stir till midnight when the barriers were cleared by the police."

There can be no doubt that, however reluctantly, the good burghers of the town took the task very seriously; if the task had to be done, it was to be done well. One of the first concerns that had faced the town's councillors was the matter of policing the execution. *The Dumfries and Galloway Police Force Order Book 1858 to 1869* records the detailed instructions given by Provost Gordon that were to be carried out.

"The Sergeants and Constables will wear their old clothing, their great coats and caps must be particularly smart and clean. They will also bring with them their cutlasses, those who have them, and their staffs and parade at English Street station at 6pm on Monday when directions will be given to them as to the nature of the duties they have to perform. The Chief Constable wishes to impress upon the minds of the men the necessity of all on duty being civil but firm in the execution of orders given to them and also to bear in mind that they must keep their temper and above all things refrain from taking intoxicating liquors. The cutlasses are to be deposited in the Chief Constables office and not be worn unless they receive special directions to do so."

The Chief Constable had mustered all the policemen he could but it had been necessary to bring in the militia and arrange to swear in two hundred special constables to supplement the small force. There were twenty eight men from the Dumfries County Constabulary, fifteen from the Stewartry County Constabulary, seven from Dumfries Burgh, and fourteen members of the militia including the captain. The police constables were instructed to wear uniform whilst the militia and the special constables were furnished with black batons. The police were told to assemble in the Court House opposite the prison at six o'clock in the morning whilst the militia and special constables were to arrive no later than seven o'clock.

The Chief Constable of Dumfries County Constabulary was given overall charge though he had to liaise with William Martin, the Town Clerk and his team to ensure that all the plans were carried into effect. The newspapers later reported that all the arrangements had been a credit to the civic authorities "who had no experience of providing for such an assemblage." One important aspect of the whole ghastly event that the town's authorities had no control over was the role of the executioner. William Calcraft was Britain's, somewhat notorious, hangman and had been since he was twenty nine in 1829, having first been employed as a flogger of juvenile offenders. Described as a squat, sturdy, hard visaged, yet mild mannered man, old in appearance with white whiskers, beard and a ruddy complexion. Although the profusion of curly iron grey hair around his face gave him a "burly countenance" he had anything but "a jolly look." He was a keen angler and rabbit fancier, but he had "a casual way with people and hanged them like dogs." At another execution Calcraft was described as going about his business "as calmly to all appearances as if he had been a tailor fitting on a coat." Hanging was, of course, his business and he made a good living from it; on top of his wages he was allowed to keep the clothing and the personal effects of his victims which he, sometimes, sold on to Madame Tussauds. Calcraft also had a reputation for using the short drop method and for miscalculating the drop required to bring about a speedy death. Only six years earlier he had made a spectacular bungle in the case of William Bousfield. [4] Even without bungling, hanging was an horrific death, the short drop method usually caused death by strangulation, the later long drop dislocating the vertebrae and also internally rupturing the jugular vein which brought about instantaneous death.

The hangman, who arrived on Monday morning by train and made straight for the prison where he remained, had been accompanied to Dumfries by a "seedy, swellish sort of bare faced fellow" who regarded himself as Calcraft's assistant but it was reported that he was a gentleman of independent means who had "taken to the business from a liking for it." Journalists reported that both men "appeared beyond excitement." On the Sunday solemn prayers were publicly offered up for the condemned prisoner in every place of worship in the town and they were followed by similar services on the following two nights, before and after the dreaded event. All the arrangements for the execution were completed by midday on Monday, apart from the erection of the gibbet.

The morning of the twenty-ninth of April 1862 "dawned thick and heavy, a dense mist resting on the houses in town and shrouding the landscape as with a winding sheet. It seemed as if Nature had put on a veil to screen her from the horrid spectacle." [5] In the first light of the

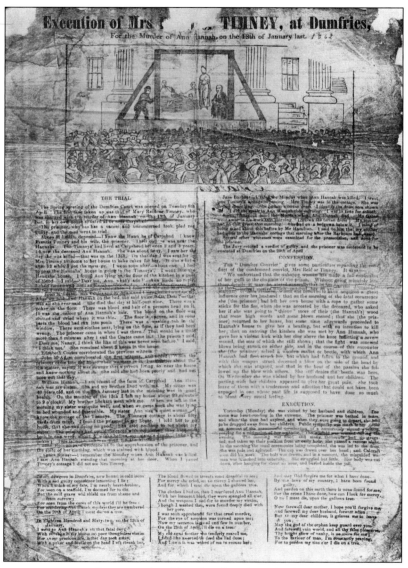

Copy of newspaper broadsheet describing the trial and execution.

morning the hideous black structure of the gallows was hoisted over the wall and erected on the scaffold, with no effort to screen the "dread machinery" from public view. As early as four in the morning, the crowd had started to gather in Buccleuch Street and the stream of people continued without stopping from that early hour until the execution was over.

Just before five o'clock Mary woke from the deep sleep induced following the hysteria of the previous evening. She appeared to be quite composed but this was due to her exhausted physical and mental state. Mary was asked if she wanted to eat but she answered that she had "last night eaten her last meal." The arrival of Rev Cowans at seven o'clock brought support and comfort but her anguish began to rise as the clock ticked by her last hour.

Outside the crowd continued to gather. It was a mixed group of people, there was a large number of women present and, as had been feared, a great number of young lads and labouring men from outside of the town. To the relief of the council and police, the crowd was smaller than they'd feared, approximately three thousand, though this was still a substantial number to be packed into the small area outside the prison (estimates in some newspapers put the figure much higher, one claiming eight thousand). "Any anticipation of a mob, indeed, was agreeably disappointed. A solemnity pervaded the crowd that, had the ghostly apparatus of death not been so apparent a passing observer might have supposed it to be a sombre religious meeting." To the credit of the town, "they behaved with great decorum, there was none of that jesting at death by shouting, catcalling and hustling each other which is said to characterise such mobs in metropolitan cities. The greatest disturbance of the peace seemed to be an itinerant preacher who with good intention no doubt had established himself among the crowd opposite the UP church and during the morning continued to harangue the masses around him in a dissonant tone of voice which fell harshly on the ear amid the comparative stillness." The same sombre aspect settled on the whole of Buccleuch Street with every householder having drawn down their window blinds as if rejecting the appalling view. "The funereal appearance of the houses, the repose of the crowd, and the general air of quiet and solemn expectation over all showed with what abhorrence the execution – however just and expedient it might be" reported *The Courier*, " was looked upon by the inhabitants of the town."

At seven o'clock Provost Gordon and the magistrates, preceded by their halberdiers, entered through the barrier at the south of Buccleuch Street and proceeded to the Court House to witness the swearing in of the special constables. The entrance to the Court House was guarded by the Militia, under the command of Captain Noake. The Provost then called upon the Rev. Mr Gray of the New Church to lead a prayer suitable for the occasion. The Town Clerk, Mr Martin took a roll call of all the constables and the Provost thanked them for answering his summons. Mr Jones, the Chief Constable of the Dumfriesshire Constabulary then took command of the force with Mr Mitchell, superintendent of the burgh police, given orders to assist if necessary. However, in an unexpected deviation from Provost Gordon's carefully laid out plans for the day, Mr McGowan, a draper, spoke up saying that he objected to the special constables being controlled by Mr Jones. Mr McGowan stated that he thought the special constables should be able to elect a captain from amongst their own ranks. The Provost agreed to this, presumably to get on with the grave matter in hand rather than bicker over such trivialities, and a surgeon dentist, Mr Pike, a colour sergeant from the Dumfries Rifle Corps, was unanimously elected to the post.

The constables then left and, along with the rural police, moved into position in an area opposite the Court House at the end of St David Street within the inner barriers. The staff of the militia, in full uniform, armed and accompanied by a bugler, were then drawn up inside the railings of the Court House. At twenty minutes from eight o'clock the Provost and Magistrates entered the prison. As part of the formal procedure Mr Martin, the Town Clerk, had drawn up a formal receipt for the living woman which was handed to the Governor of the prison and in return Mary was given into the custody of the burgh. A reporter with *The Glasgow Daily Herald*, who had been able to accompany the group into the prison, later reported that they "heard the loud and prolonged moaning of the wretched being resounding through the building telling of her extreme misery."

The officials then came out into the open space in Buccleuch Street where the Rev Mr Gray had taken up his position at the entrance to Mr T H McGowan's residence next door to the Court House, a place where he could be seen by the crowd. The singing of four verses of the fifty-first psalm, traditionally associated with confession and renewal but also known as 'the necking verse' in hanging circles, was led by a Mr Wright, the precentor of the New Church. The newspapers reported that "the plaintive notes of the tune, St Paul's, rose in mournful and solemnising cadence above the suppressed hum of the crowds outside the barriers." There were further prayers and singing, and as the last line ended the clock struck eight. The Provost and the magistrates, accompanied by several police commissioners, then re-entered the prison. The magistrates proceeded to the court yard where there was a clear view of the scaffold.

As the solemn ceremony of the event went on outside the prison walls, the little time that Mary had left, as Lord Deas had so harshly told her at the end of her trial, was now counted in minutes, not hours. With her was the chaplain, her support and comfort for the past three weeks. He read a chapter from the bible and then suggested some thoughts for her arising from the passage before praying with her. She was again, "agonised with fear," and any spoken words were focussed on her children and the dreadful death that was drawing near. At eight o'clock the executioner Calcraft went to prepare her for the gibbet, pinioning her arms in a contraption he'd invented a decade earlier. Mary's arms were pinioned by way of a broad leather body-belt which was clasped round the waist and to this the arm straps were fastened. Two inch and a half wide straps with strong buckles clasp the elbows while another similar strap went round the wrists. Mary had been moved into a small cell in a passage that ended with a window leading out onto the scaffold. The poor woman had, understandably, lost whatever composure she had gained over the previous weeks from her visits from the chaplain. As Calcraft, accompanied by two assistants, prepared her for her execution, she would have been able to hear the solemn voices of the thousands outside in the streets singing, waiting to witness her very public death.

As the singing ended and a subdued quiet came over the crowd they heard Mary's cries for the first time. From inside the prison came the loud shrieks of a woman clearly in abject terror, her tortured screams echoing down the passageway as she was led out by Calcraft with Mr Cowans "whose kind ministrations followed her even to the drop" and Mr Stewart, the prison Governor, helping her on this final walk. "Her cries, which were most heart-rending, ranged through the empty corridors and cells and must have been distinctly heard by the other inmates of the prison. Even then, when death was staring her in the face she declared that she had not murdered Ann Hannah and that it was Ann Hannah that had struck her first. She moaned and cried piteously and besought them not to hang her as she was only a young woman."

As the dignitaries and crowd caught sight of Mary for the first time they were struck to the heart by her distress and appearance. She was wearing a simple lilac calico dress, a tartan shawl and a white 'mutch' with a capacious frill.[6] In the few weeks since the trial her appearance had changed enormously. "The prisoner seemed in a frantic and distracted state. The crushing agony of the last three weeks seemed to have had a great effect upon both mind and body. Her countenance had lost all the firmness, stolidity or stupidity which it wore during the trial and was pale, vacant and distorted with terror; fear of some great and incomprehensible danger was impressed on every lineament and she seemed to have grown twenty years older since the day of her trial. When she reached the open air she gazed round her and looked up to the blue sky and the objects around her with a kind of idiotic, maniacal or hysterical stare. It was remarked in our hearing that she had become insane and had it not been for the words she uttered in her great distress it would have been difficult to convince us that the 'lamp of reason had not wavered and gone out.' She screamed aloud in tones that brought a shudder to the hearts of those who heard her 'oh no, oh no, oh my four weans, oh my four weans!'" Other observers said that she was "so pale, so worn with her sufferings that instead of looking like a woman of twenty-seven she looked far more like a old woman of seventy. Her cheeks were sunk; her head was bent down, though occasionally she reared it suddenly up to take a wild survey of the crowd below."

As if there had not been enough drama and horror in the whole case, Mary had just been brought out on to the platform where the gibbet stood when a cry of 'stop' was heard from a breathless messenger hurrying into the court yard with a letter. For a moment there was an hesitation, a hope that the message contained some kind of pardon or commutation of the sentence and this horrible spectacle would, after all, not go ahead. It was widely known that Mrs McCulloch had written to Sir George Grey again on the previous Saturday, begging him to reconsider. "The eyes of those who witnessed its delivery were riveted upon Mr Stewart and recollections of reprieves to prisoners when on the scaffold flashed like electricity through the minds of everyone." But the paper was crushed and with a disdainful toss, cast aside by the prison governor who was heard to shout "Go on." It would be later revealed that it had been a request from a Mr J H Butterfield, a London editor urgently asking for the particulars of the execution to be telegraphed to him in time for the evening edition of his newspaper.

This final flurry of dashed hope seemed to drain from Mary what little strength she had left and she had to be lifted step by step towards the gibbet by Calcraft's two assistants, the tops of their shining silk hats were the first things to appear above the parapet. Catching sight of the officials standing in the court yard, Mary imploringly cried "my four weans", "uttering the cry in accents most piteous and heart rending." At the sight of her the spell of solemnity that had held the crowd seemed to break and it was replaced by wailing cries of pity and commiseration that "rose like a great sigh in the morning air."

Mary continued her plaintive appeals and asked to stand a moment as Calcraft, with his white bushy beard and black velvet skull cap, busied himself with his preparations with the noose and coil of new rope he had carried with him onto the scaffold. She had to be supported again as the executioner with "great coolness and deliberation" took off her mutch and instead drew a white cap, that he took out of his pocket, down over her face and tied her legs. The cap, shaped really like a bag, was white to be in contrast with the judge's black cap and a woman's legs were tied to prevent her skirts billowing up. Instead of finding a crook at the end of his rope to link it to the beam above, Calcraft had to call for a pair of steps which he then climbed in order to tie the rope to the beam, an operation that took a full two minutes whilst the poor woman, the white hood drawn over her face, stood shivering and sobbing unable to understand the delay. Some of the crowd at this point became anxious to get away, regretting their presence at this awful scene but moments later the two men who had supported Mary up the steps now, assisted by Calcraft, lifted her onto the narrow trapdoor, still crying and calling for her children. "The mother's feeling was the strongest" wrote *The Glasgow Daily Herald* "even in death" though her words had become muffled and incomprehensible beneath the white hood.

"He adjusted the noose upon her neck," *The Standard* reported "fastened the rope to the cross bean and at twenty three minutes past eight o'clock, drew the bolt." *The Glasgow Daily Herald* said that as Mary felt the "drop jacking beneath her while the bolt was being drawn" she let out a "louder muffled scream but the scream was cut short in the middle; before it was finished she was swinging in the air." *The Standard* said that "the unfortunate woman dropped fifteen inches. Death, to all appearances was painless and easy and the executioner, who must be allowed to be a good judge in such matters, said she died instantly. She only gave one desperate convulsive struggle after the drop fell and the twitching of the fingers apparent for some time after life was extinct was supposed to arise solely from nervous or muscular action." When the bolt was drawn there was 'a thrill of horror' that chilled every heart and one of the officials in the court yard almost fainted whilst two of the militia collapsed, literally falling out of rank. A cry of great distress rose from the crowds on both sides of the barriers "as if the ground had been swallowing them up."

"The body, a hideous spectacle in the calm, blue sunny April morning hung fully thirty minutes – the customary time – exposed to the gaze of the vulgar crowds on the streets from whom solitary cries of pain and distress arose at intervals. As the body hung on the gibbet the mist lifted and the sun shone out brightly. At five minutes from nine o'clock the corpse was lowered into the arms of officers in waiting and carried into the prison. The crowds quietly dispersed, the special constables gave up their batons and at ten o'clock the town had regained its ordinarily quiet aspect but the unspeakable horror of that awful morning scene will haunt and harass the minds of the onlookers." It was reported that Mary's face had a "placid aspect of the features – colourless and calm as if no violence had been done – showing that death had been momentary and accompanied with but little pain." At three o'clock Mary's body was placed in a simple pine coffin and, watched over by various officials, buried within the precincts of the prison.

The following day, an editorial in *The Dumfries Standard*, concluded: "Truly this tragedy of Carsphad has been a dreadful business from beginning to end: the chief actor in it has died many deaths and the most sanguinary had 'supposed horrors' enough from it without being surfeited and causing the general public to be shocked with the scene yesterday between the obvious finisher of the law and his maniacal victim."

Ten

"was swung and strangled between heaven and earth the body of a woman, a wife and a mother."

Just as Provost Gordon had feared the name of Dumfries was on the lips of many people across the nation as reports of the execution appeared in just about every newspaper in Britain and Ireland. A public hanging had become something of a rarity by the middle of the century, and especially the hanging of a woman. Some newspapers like *The Carlisle Examiner* ran special supplements and, of course, the execution itself had suffered an ill timed delay due to the eagerness of one London editor. Cities with a large Irish population like Liverpool and Dundee took a particular interest. Whilst all the coverage spoke of the horror of this public spectacle there was some comfort for the people and officials of Dumfries in the praise expressed for the sympathetic and dignified way it had been carried out. *The Belfast News Letter* said "the quiet conduct of the crowd and and the seemliness with which the sad and tragic affair passed off was a matter of some congratulations amongst the inhabitants of Dumfries who had dreaded a scene of confusion."

Remnants of the thousands who had witnessed Mary's death waited to follow the hangman Calcraft to the station. *The Courier* said that there was "nothing more revolting than the businesslike coolness" of the executioner. He was booed and jostled along his walk from Buccleuch Street to the station at Lover's Walk to catch the 11.25 train to London. It was reported that the "old gentleman had a blooming wallflower in his black coat breast and took all the hissing and hooting in good part" receiving all this attention with "imperturbable composure." Calcraft had, by then, been the hangman for more than thirty years, of what would be a forty five year career, and was well used to being subjected to this kind of hostile treatment from crowds.

Although all the newspapers were clear about Mary's guilt, there was widespread horror that the public hanging of a young woman had gone ahead. *The Liverpool Echo* wrote "With an almost imperceptible twitch of her body, and a slight elevation of her hands, Mary Timney – woman, a wife and mother – expiated her crime with an awful penalty and has done with human laws and human vengeance". One London weekly title wrote "was swung and strangled between heaven and earth the body of a woman, a wife and a mother."

Whilst the main campaigning for the reprieve had been led by *The Dumfries Standard*, the paper was by no means alone in its view of the case. In May *The Walsall Free Press* called for Lord Deas' retirement from the bench arguing that the production of the children in court had shown how weak the case was and that "never was a poor wretch convicted on such slender evidence. We have carefully watched this case from the commencement of its history to its barbarous and bloody termination and cannot find a single excuse for the Home Office withholding from the unfortunate Mary Reid or Timney, that mercy extended to the Bilston murders. The latter – adepts in crime – enter the house of their victim for unlawful purpose and were therefore to all intents and purposes responsible for what afterward transpired." [1]

In Dundee, the city's newspapers had also closely followed the events in Dumfries. *The Dundee Standard* expressed disgust at the proceedings of the trial and in particular the treatment of Mary's daughter Susan. "Not only did the Advocate depute endeavour to extort answers from her condemnatory to the prisoner but the judge pressed the questions most persistently. His Lordship presumably supposed that the child would say something about the mallet but the little witness, a very pretty girl, withstood the combined assault. Those present could not but admire the resolution of the child. There is something radically wrong in a law which sets natural affections and truth in opposition to each other. The recent law which allows the child to become a witness against its parent is not wise and we cannot but think that in this case it was pressed with undue severity."

Also in Dundee, a leading minister decided to make the Timney case the subject of his popular monthly lecture. The Reverend George Gilfillan was an author and poet who had been ordained as a pastor of a secessionist church in 1836. As a preacher and lecturer he regularly drew large crowds to his church at School Wynd, and this sermon was subsequently widely reported by the press.

"My friends you may tremble and tremble justly at God's judgements; but oh! His judgement is often far less harsh and severe than the judgement of man. And need I refer in proof of this to that event which has shed a shudder of horror through every sensitive soul in Scotland – to the execution in Dumfries. I have always been an enemy of capital punishments. I oppose them because they are barbarous and bloody relics of a bloody and brutal past. I oppose them because they are useless expenditure of human life which have never been proved to deter from a career in crime – never proved to have prevented a single murder. They tend to enthrone Revenge instead of Justice and an Almighty Fiend instead of a an All Wise and All Merciful God, a tendency to harden the human heart and brutify the human race and to degrade human nature to its core.

"Conceive a young woman of twenty seven, the mother of four children – who under great provocation with her passions stirred and boiling to the greatest point of intensity but with no premeditation – no premeditation that has at least been proved – killing her neighbour. Conceive that young woman protesting her innocence of murderous intention to the very last – protesting with the solemn asserverations that she had no intention beforehand to murder her victim, but only of expressing her injured feelings and roused passions against her. See that woman, after several sleepless nights and a fasting morning, brought out

93

at last to be deprived of life and on what are her thoughts fixed? Is she filled with remorse for her crime? No, all her thoughts, all her feelings are at home! Her whole soul is brooding over, is yearning over, her children and she says again and again in language that must have pierced the hearts around her – unless they had been hearts of adamant – unless they had been hearts as hard as those of the legal lord who condemned her – she says 'oh my puir, puir weans! What will become of them?' At last the gallows – the hideous gallows – looming up as if fresh from hell, which no doubt the idea of it first came – at last the gallows appear in view. She shrinks back in horror – she tries to stop but no! She is told that she must go on and had she stopped another moment she would have been dragged on by main force. And then at last – still without one word acknowledging her guilt, and still with her whole soul yearning with material tenderness over her poor motherless children – this woman expires by that horrible and shameful death."

The congregation was already deeply moved by his words and newspapers reported that many women were left sobbing. The harrowing event certainly prompted debate and it would remain in the minds of the people of Dumfries, the execution fuelling the fury many felt rather than bring a sense of completion to the sorry tale. Two of the town's newspapers viewed aspects of the case from politically opposing positions. *The Courier* repeatedly reported justifications for the execution and continued its more macabre interest in the event publishing the information that not only had Mary's body been left to hang for half an hour but that after being taken down people were allowed to view it, many reporting that she did not have the tortured disfigurement that often featured on the faces of the hanged. "Those who had the courage or curiosity to view the corpse after it had been cut down from the gibbet concur in stating that the countenance wore a calm, peaceful and even pleasing expression, there being not the slightest distortion or discolouration, all going to show that death had been instantaneous and unaccompanied by much physical agony." All this somewhat grisly information must have come as something of a relief for the Provost and his staff given Calcraft's reputation for using the, not always straightforward, short drop method.

William McDowall, the editor of *The Standard*, took no comfort in such details and could barely restrain his obvious rage: "Our sole object is to extract some useful moral from this atrocious exhibition; for if, to the intelligent mind, disease and death and putrescence and pollution be pregnant with instruction it may happen that from so hateful a sight as the public strangling of Mary Reid or Timney, a beneficial public lesson may be extracted." Although in reality, the appeals to the Queen had for many years been decided by the Home Secretary, this had, perhaps, not been fully understood by the public and the realisation of the situation prompted a hard hitting article by the outraged Mr McDowall: "It is generally believed that her Gracious Majesty the Queen is a legal power in the land and that in this respect her personality is not quite absorbed by ministerial officialism. Her Majesty is frequently spoken of as the Fountain of Justice and Mercy, and many people for this reason think that the Sovereign is, at all events, made conversant with important judicial cases which involve life and death and that petitions from her subjects regarding such cases are really laid at the foot of the Throne and duly considered by its royal and illustrious occupant. This fond idea has been rudely dispelled in the South of Scotland by the treatment given to the petitions from Dumfries and other towns in the district on behalf of the miserable woman whose life was yesterday taken by the executioner. These petitions were correct in point of form, most respectfully worded and their prayer for a commutation of sentence was backed by several weighty representations; but they were not laid before the Queen: the ponderous petitions bearing the names of at least six thousand of Her Majesty's loyal subjects, were cast into Mr Waddington's waste basket at the Home Office, and the prayer they breathed was never once named to Her Majesty and up till this present hour the Queen, we believe, has been kept in utter ignorance of the case to which the petitions refer.

"There was one petition in particular which deserved better usage – the one signed by 3187 females in favour of the criminal, who, though fallen to the lowest depths, they still recognised as a fitting object of compassion and towards whom they earnestly besought the Queen to show mercy. This unique document was, like all the rest, intercepted in its passage to the Throne. Red tape stood in the way; state etiquette frowned upon it and so, instead of being submitted to the Sovereign it was coldly consigned to the Lethean depositories of the Home Department. It would be a vile prostitution of language to say that the Queen refused to listen to the prayer of the petitioners. It was never allowed to reach her gracious ear, if it had, who shall say that it would not have been anxiously considered or that the answer given to it would have been pitiless, like that of Her Majesty's representative, Sir George Grey? The petitioners embodied a constitutional appeal from the decision of the Circuit Court to the Crown as the highest tribunal in the country; but in this instance there was a deplorable anticlimax from the jewelled round of sovereignty to the horse hair wig of the judge, for instead of the appeal being carried to the Fountain of mercy it was laid before the inexorable justicians whose decision it sought to set aside, and whose charge on a very material part of the evidence had been challenged as unwarranted by many of the petitioners. When the Home Secretary adopted such a course it was not to be supposed in the nature of things, that the death sentence would be interfered with – the only hope for the petitioners and the miserable object of their care having been that the minister would either allow her case to be brought before the Queen personally or decide it himself after consultation with the principal law authorities irrespective of Lord Deas."

Of course it must be noted that Queen Victoria had only very recently lost her husband, Prince Albert who died unexpectedly in December 1861. The Queen had been overwhelmed by grief, coming so soon after the death of her mother, and she had withdrawn from public life and matters of state, a situation that went on for far longer than anyone would have imagined and may not have been fully appreciated by the public at the time.

Mr McDowall wrote of his deep regret that the case had not been "fully or fairly reconsidered." He argued that by pointing to the Queen's recent bereavement people were underrating her "strength of mind, her concern for the good of her subjects and her special solicitude for the fallen and the miserable." *The Standard* had no qualms at pointing to the figure it felt was to blame for this outrage that had occurred in the streets of Dumfries – Sir George Grey. "The Home Secretary had the power of preventing the scandal. This power he has declined to exert. In sight of God and man the Home Secretary is blameable for the outrage upon the taste and feelings of society involved in the public, deliberate and cold blooded strangling of Mary Timney. Sir George Grey is true to the reputation which he already richly earned as the most remorseless and pitiless Home Minister England ever had within the memory of a living generation. It is this unconquerable determination to find full employment for Mr Calcraft which has earned Sir George Grey the title of The Hanging Secretary than which no truer discriminating appellation ever was bestowed for verily the Home Secretary is the gallows' greatest purveyor."

The argument of many abolitionists that cases such as that of Mary Timney often achieved the opposite effect intended by the hideous spectacle of a public execution, was repeated by Mr McDowall. The law had became loathsome to the public, "the safety of life and property imperilled by enlisting against the institution which punishes crime the public indignation which ought to be directed against the criminal. All that an earthly tribunal has to do is to to prevent the recurrence of the crime – to inspire and maintain in the individual public mind, a strong and unconquerable loathing of the offence. But it is self evident when the sympathies of the community at large are enlisted on the side of the offender that this end is frustrated. In regard to Mary Timney, this has been the case."

From the moment when the judge pronounced the death sentence the piteous appeal for mercy from Mary had resulted in a profound effect upon those in court followed by men and women of all classes in and around Dumfries who had "exerted themselves to the utmost of their power in order to obtain a commutation of the capital sentence. Deputations composed of the most respectable and influential inhabitants of the borough and county attended at the Home Office, petitions, memorials to which thousands of signatures were readily procured all entreating that the wretched woman should not be strangled but some other punishment more in harmony with the spirit of the age should be inflicted on her. But all in vain."

For campaigners like William Ewart the punishment of hanging was barbarous, brutal and ineffectual because of its demoralising effect on public feeling, the taking of human life by the State rendering it less not more secure. *The Standard* editor wrote: "Nothing is now more undoubted than that every public execution sows the seeds of future murders broadcast over the land. Calcraft is the licensed state professor of homicide and Sir George Grey seems determined that this great public teacher shall not lack subjects for the constitution of his detestable institution."

The letters page of *The Dumfries Standard* in the edition following Mary's execution was filled with the outrage of local people including one clergyman who said he had become more and more convinced that her life should have been spared; "the poor creature suffered a hundred deaths and probably her crime was not so cold blooded after all." Like many others he urged something to be done to support the 'four weans' that had been Mary's main concern and the last words on her lips.

Mr Ewart added his voice: "The more I have considered the question, the more I felt convinced that her reprieve might have been justifiably granted. It is not enough to shew that an accused person may have gone with the intent to murder. It should be shewn directly or circumstantially that she (or he) must have gone with that intent. The case had excited considerable attention here and many members of the House of Commons have expressed to me their surprise and regret that the prerogative of mercy was not exercised." Mr Ewart referred to the cases of two women who had been proven to have committed murder, Annette Meyer and Celestina Somners, and yet both had been reprieved. Annette Meyer was a young woman who shot her seducer, a soldier, after she was abandoned by him when she ran out of money and refused to prostitute herself to earn more. In Meyer's case, heard in February 1847, there had been a considerable amount of damning evidence against her from the shopkeeper who sold her the pistol through to people she had told of her plan to shoot the former lover. She was found guilty but the jury strongly recommended mercy due to the extraordinary provocation and ill treatment she had been subjected to. Although sentenced to death for this crime which was motivated by jealousy or revenge, the sentence was commuted by Sir George Grey to two years imprisonment followed by transportation.

A further case, contemporaneous with Mary's, brought to the attention of Dumfries readers, was that of an Inverness man battered to death by a hammer blow with a man, his wife and daughter all suspected of the crime though the daughter, Isabella Ferguson, was the only one brought to trial. It was argued that drink had contributed to the man's death and the defence advocate referred to the girl's poor upbringing and drunken mother. She had been given a sentence of just eighteen months in prison and it was reported that the judge had regretted that he could not make the sentence less. *The Dumfries Standard* wrote "I wish Mary Timney had come before Lords Neave and Ardmillan as I believe she would have been given a penalty of imprisonment, escaping the bloodthirsty vengeance that has dishonoured the law and made our community sick and sore at heart."

A letter signed 'Justicia' continued the argument that the legal case against Mary had been highly flawed. "*The Courier* asserts, I presume, as an excuse for Lord Deas' fatal misdirection of the jury, that there is no moral doubt that Mary Timney carried the mallet with her to Ann Hannah's. I this day saw one of the legal gentlemen who precognosed Mary Timney's children at the first and he positively declared that the children stated that their mother did not carry anything with her in her hand when she went to Ann Hannah's on the fatal occasion. But suppose she had carried the mallet with her, then so much the worse for Lord Deas as it would be a prima facie evidence that his mind had been filled and biased by statements other than the evidence produced in court, a thing which almost every judge and advocate warns the jury to beware of as being contrary to Law and Justice." [2]

Many shared the views of Mr McDowall that if the "manifold disadvantages," of the way Mary's case was submitted and the reality of "her evil surroundings since childhood" had been presented to the Queen, there would have been a different result to the petitions. "The case at the worst seems to us to have been one of those which lie on the boundary line between cold-blooded deliberate murder and culpable homicide and the circumstance of the woman and the trial ought to have been put into the scale in her favour and the sentence reduced to one of a secondary nature in deference to those considerations and to the enlightened and merciful character of the age." *The Belfast News Letter* did not share his opinion though, saying instead that the "pitiable compound of malignity and selfishness shown in the murder and the subsequent impeachment of her own mother have given the crime of the woman Timney an enduring place in the criminal annals of Scotland."

In contrast such was the feeling in Dumfries about what had happened to Mary Timney that one man was prompted to write to the papers to plead his own innocence. A Thomas Shenan wrote denying that he had been responsible for digging Mary Timney's grave. Such were the rumours in the town that he had been the grave digger that, as a result, he had been unable to find work since the execution.

Despite the indignation at the perceived injustice of Mary's case and the horror of the execution itself, some good did come out of the episode.

Nationally William Ewart was inspired to make one final attempt at abolishing capital punishment and on a local level, the lives of Mary's four children were changed. In May the Dumfries press reported that from Kells, Mary's own parish, an idea had been put forward that the children should be given an education provided that a sufficient sum could be raised from the public. Subscription papers were made available at the Bank of Scotland, the British Linen Company, the National, the Royal and the Union Banks in Dumfries and the agents Mr Johnson, Mr Adamson, Hannay and McKie, Gordon and Whitelaw, Jackson and Symons had all agreed to take charge of the sums subscribed which would be forwarded to the Rev Dr James Maitland, Minister of Kells. The idea was "warmly taken up by the people of Dumfries and district."

Eleven

"Demonised or deemed insane – they must be mad or bad"

Life in the south west was just beginning to return to a quiet rural routine after the disruption and distress of the Glenkens murder and its aftermath when the issues of the case were, once again, ignited. In July a dreadful murder was committed in Glasgow that drew comparisons with the Timney case; a woman had been killed and another younger woman arrested, though she denied the charge and blamed someone else. Twenty eight year old Jessie McLachlan, a young married mother, was accused of murdering an older friend, thirty five year old Jess McPherson who was a servant in the household of a respectable accountant, John Fleming. His elderly father James, known as Old Fleming, was initially arrested and although he was released, McLachlan continued to accuse the old man of the crime and many believed that he was somehow implicated if not guilty. Like Mary Timney, Jessie McLachlan gave a series of differing, lengthy statements explaining various aspects of the evidence that appeared to tie her to the crime. In his book Square Mile of Murder, Jack House said that some people described her as a pathological liar whilst others said she was a panic-stricken woman in a desperate situation. The Glasgow papers, *The Herald* and *The Morning Journal*, took opposing views of the case and the judge presiding over the trial was once again Lord Deas.

After three days of evidence the jury deliberated for only fifteen minutes before bringing a unanimous verdict of guilty. Before Lord Deas donned the black cap, something he had ostentatiously carried into the trial the press noted, Jessie McLachlan asked for a statement to be read to the court in which she gave yet another lengthy version of the murder. Lord Deas remained unmoved and sentenced her to be hanged on the eleventh of October 1862. Just as in the Timney case, a large number of people believed that, although the woman was certainly implicated in the crime, she was innocent of the charge of murder and a petition process began to try and delay the execution until more enquiries into the case could be made. Years later the Sheriff of Lanarkshire, Sir Archibald Alison wrote in his autobiography words which could easily have been applied to Mary's case; "She had not a fair trial; the minds of the jury were made up before they entered the box. This was proved by their bringing a verdict in fifteen minutes where the evidence had occupied three days. There was a miscarriage of justice; but it arose from the publicity of their proceedings not their secrecy."

A mass meeting was held in Glasgow City Hall in late September at which it was claimed that 50,000 signatures had been gathered for the petition and the following day on the instructions of the Lord Advocate a process of investigation and enquiry began which resulted in a reprieve. Jessie McLachlan was instead order to be imprisoned for the term of her natural life and she served fifteen years at Perth prison before being released on a ticket of leave in October 1877, coincidentally the same year as Lord Deas died. A year after the murder McLachlan issued a fifth statement about the crime which differed again from all of her previous declarations, this time she admitted that she had been at the scene but insisting that Old Fleming had carried out the killing whilst she had been intoxicated on a mixture of drink and laudanum.

Whilst some commentators were appalled at the reprieve others were furious that, given the similarities of the two cases, Mary Timney had not been treated in the same way. As a metropolitan crime, The Sandyford Murder, as it was known, had received even greater press coverage than the Carsphad or Glenkens Murder and it had been hotly debated in newspapers throughout Scotland and beyond. The similarities of the two cases were not lost on the people of the south west and in Dumfries *The Standard* editor was enraged. He felt it had been made clear to the Home Secretary that in the Timney trial, "Lord Deas had misdirected the jury on a vital portion of the evidence; that the prisoner's case from beginning to end was mismanaged; that there was a strong reason to believe that the fatal blow was unpremeditated; and that there were many mitigating circumstances such as the woman's mental weakness, ignorance, excitability and the provocation received by her which ought to have told in her favour." Yet "the right honourable baronet set all such considerations aside." *The Standard* claimed that Sir George Grey had been "assured by Lord Deas that the prisoner's version of the murder was 'a tissue of falsehoods'" and so did not venture "in the interests of mercy" to run counter to the judge's opinion. If the Home Secretary had followed the same course as he had just a few months later in the Jessie McLachlan case, the Dumfries paper believed that it would have provided an opportunity to get "fresh evidence for the prisoner which she had been unable, on account of her poverty and friendlessness, to bring forward to the trial." In November 1862, *The Standard* demanded to know what had brought about the change in the "heart of the minister towards" Jessie McLachlan when he had so callously ignored "powerful extenuating circumstances" in Mary Timney's case.

The widespread interest in the events following the trial of Jessie McLachlan led to an interesting revelation at a meeting of the Dumfries Town Council when the case came under discussion; Provost Gordon was prompted to make a surprising comment about the circumstances of Mary Timney's trial and execution. He informed the councillors that when he became aware that the Carsphad case would come before the circuit court in Dumfries, fearing that "a very disagreeable duty might devolve on the town's magistrates," he had made it his business when Lord Deas arrived in town, to ask his Lordship, the advocate depute and the clerk, if it was possible for the scaffold to be erected in another town; he personally favoured Kirkcudbright. Lord Deas, however, had ruled that it should take place in Dumfries. This information was widely reported but it is clear from the tone of the article in *The Kirkcudbright Advertiser* that their main focus was their shock that the Provost had been intent on avoiding the expense and shame of the hideous spectacle by getting the execution held in their small town. The report failed to mention the more obvious concern that was expressed by a councillor McGowan who said he hoped he'd misunderstood what he'd heard and asked for clarification. The Provost confirmed that the conversation he'd had with the judge had been on the day before the trial. Councillor McGowan said that he thought the Provost had put the judge in "a very awkward position" but Mr Gordon was indignant, claiming that the gentlemen had shown "a total want of information on the point on which he had consulted them" because they had said they "were not aware of any precedent but promised to tell him if there was a precedent for such a thing to be done."

The Kirkcudbright Advertiser reported that even after the execution the Provost had not been satisfied in the matter and thought it was a "great hardship that Dumfries should have been saddled with it and that in addition the burgh should be immersed in heavy expense." He'd continued his mission with zeal and when in Edinburgh at the General Assembly he discovered that holding an execution in a different place to the trial had occurred in several other cases, including Ayr, though on that occasion the sentence had been commuted. [1] At the Town Council meeting Provost Gordon expressed his astonishment that Lord Deas and the Advocate Depute had not known this and so he was pleased to be able to report that after a lengthy correspondence with the authorities in Edinburgh, the Town Clerk Mr Martin had been able to get a refund for Dumfries for all the expenses involved in the execution, short of £23, though they had every intention of claiming this back from Kirkcudbright Town Council. The Provost was applauded by some councillors for his commitment to his duties but *The Dundee Advertiser's* report of the meeting picked up on the point that councillor McGowan had attempted to make – that it had been inappropriate to have had the conversation at all before Mary had even been tried. The Dundee paper commented: "There can be little question, we think, of the Provost's zeal for the interests of the burgh, but Lord Deas might, with all propriety, have told him that he had better "nurse his zeal to keep it warm" until he saw whether the woman was to be executed at all or not."

Despite Lord Deas' propensity towards the death sentence he wasn't always so harsh towards the accused, especially if they happened to be middle class and male. Five years after the Timney and McLachlan cases he sat in judgement at the trial of a well connected military man who had retired from the Indian Army. Alexander Dingwall, a man described as being "irreclaimably addicted to drink" had murdered his wife with a carving knife after she had hidden his supply of alcohol and money at Hogmanay.[2] Lord Deas instructed the jury that although the accused could not be found insane they could return a verdict of culpable homicide due to "weak mindedness" because his "intoxicated state" could have been an indication of diminished responsibility. In her book *Certain Other Countries, Homicide, Gender and National Identity*, historian Carolyn Conley states that this case not only set a precedent for accepting drunkenness as a form of mitigation but it also illustrated that "in Scotland diminished responsibility seemed to be available primarily to the well connected" and "the social status of the accused was an important factor in determining trial outcomes."

Of course Mary was of the lowest social standing and had no-one, let alone someone well connected, to call upon before the trial. Mary, it seems, was unlucky on many levels. Between 1800 and 1868 two hundred and seventy three people were publicly hanged in Scotland, two hundred and fifty nine men and only fourteen women. A further two hundred and seven people were sentenced but either reprieved or respited.[3] Scottish death sentences were the least likely to be carried out. Only thirty four per cent of the condemned in Scotland were executed and over half of the death sentences that were commuted had been based on unanimous verdicts.[4] Mary's poverty was clearly a factor in Lord Deas unsympathetic view of her case and her gender probably added to his distaste for the crime she had committed. Beatrix Campbell, in her foreword to Ann Jones' book *Women Who Kill* states that "the woman who kills is exactly what she is supposed not to be. Her act is deemed not only unnatural but impossible in a real woman; so she is 'unwomaned' by her violence and seen as a classic aberration, exiled from her community and her gender." In *Men of Blood, Violence, Manliness and Criminal Justice in Victorian England*, author Martin J Wiener wrote that "killing a wife's sexual partner was not exonerated in Victorian courts but was dealt with comparatively leniently. Fighting and other uses of violence were viewed as almost a normal part of men's lives and the fact of a man killed by another man was less shocking than that of a murdered woman." He also stated, though, that if the fact of a murdered woman was highly shocking, so too was that of a woman's execution "not only juries but even judges bent over backwards to avoid hanging women." Again, Mary appears to have been particularly unfortunate in getting a judge who, instead, seemed to have decided the sentence even before he stepped in the court if his conversation with the Dumfries Provost is any indication of intent.

Seen against a backdrop of Carolyn Conley's extensive research in the archives of murder in the United Kingdom Mary's case is thrown into sharp relief at every turn. Lower class Scots were more likely to be executed than the upper classes and Scottish women had a higher rate of conviction for homicide outside their immediate family than either sex in any other part of the United Kingdom. They were also twenty per cent more likely to be convicted than Scotsmen. Violent women created a particular challenge for the courts and the press as "they so clearly violated gender definitions." Given that feminist historians have suggested that women who killed had to be "demonised or deemed insane – they must be mad or bad" it is even more remarkable in the case of Mary Timney, that after the trial there was so much public support for the commutation of her sentence, from her own community and even from the murder victim's own brother.

The fact that the petitioners, backed by an array of political heavyweights, did not succeed begs the question why was the sentence not commuted when compared to other similar cases from the same period like Isabella Ferguson, Jessie McLachlan and fellow Glaswegian, Roseanne Simpson. In comparison Mary was judged harshly. Simpson was accused of beating a neighbour to death with some bellows because the woman had taunted her about being childless. Simpson admitted hitting her but witnesses at the case testified to the provocation she had suffered and Simpson was found guilty of assault and sentenced to four months in prison.[5] According to Carolyn Conley, women provoked by jealousy sometimes received the support of judges as in the case of Margaret McDonald, another resident of Glasgow, who had killed a woman she believed was flirting with her husband in "a frenzy of passion" after first torturing her for an hour. At the conclusion of her trial in 1889 she was sentenced to ten years imprisonment after Justice Young decided that crime was "just short of murder." Conley's research shows that between 1867 and 1892 there were three hundred and fifty trials of women accused of killing someone other than a spouse, child or step child and of those only twenty nine were convicted of murder.

Whilst it appears that gender, class, poverty and certainly the misfortune of being judged by Lord Deas were all factors in Mary being sentenced to death, the refusal of Sir George Grey to commute her sentence to imprisonment even after her confession, the petitions, the high profile support and the legal questions about the trial still begs the question why he showed no compassion towards her case?

The Wigtownshire Free Press said: "It has been a dreadful end to a degraded life and forms another solemn illustration of the truth of the Divine word, the wages of sin is … death. May it be the last spectacle of its kind which will ever be witnessed either in Dumfries or anywhere else in the south of Scotland."

Twelve

"A fragment of mediaeval barbarism."

On the eleventh of May 1868 the third reading was held in parliament of the *Capital Punishment (Amendment) Act*, the result of a Royal Commission instigated by Dumfries MP William Ewart. On the same day nineteen year old Robert Smith, convicted of raping and murdering a young girl, became the last man to be publicly hanged in Scotland, again in Dumfries. At the end of the month the Act came into force bringing an end to public executions, but for Ewart this was not a reason for celebration.

Although William Ewart's name, as a Radical, will always be associated with the campaign for the education of the working classes and the establishment of public libraries one issue was always at the core of his political career – the abolition of capital punishment. He raised the matter regularly during his more than thirty years as a parliamentarian. Born in Liverpool, the son of a merchant banker, the Ewarts were descended from an old Galloway family and his grandfather had been a minister of the Church of Scotland living in Troqueer in Dumfries. Ewart's focus always remained on trying to achieve the complete abolition of the death sentence but he realised very early in his career as a Member of Parliament that the only chance of succeeding was by stealth. Before the Whigs gained power in the 1830 election the previous Home Secretary, Robert Peel, had strongly defended the death sentence and let more people hang than any other incumbent during the previous hundred years. Ewart, as a new independent, abolitionist MP, along with this colleagues Fitzroy Kelly and John Bright, was determined to bring about change. In the House of Commons in March 1832 he rose to move to abolish capital punishment for stealing horses, cattle and sheep and stealing from a dwelling house 'no person being in fear therein.' This success was followed in 1834 by an end to hanging the executed in chain. According to the author of *The Hanging Tree*, V A C Gatrell, it was "Ewart who put the heaviest pressure on Lord John Russell to begin the repeals of capital statutes in 1837 and it was he too, who in March 1840 first invited the Commons to abolish capital punishment completely." Ewart tried to persuade the House of Commons that society had a right to inflict such an amount of punishment as was necessary to its safety and preservation – but no more. He argued that capital punishment was irrevocable and it diminished the public respect for human life. Although he was unsuccessful he had gained the support of ninety votes, unthinkable before 1832. Ewart then backed Fitzroy Kelly's attempt to further reduce the number of crimes punishable by death but by the time the bill gained its Royal Assent in June 1841 it was just a shadow of the original proposal, though been a step forward. In his Act of 1836 Ewart also established the right of defence counsels to sum up before a jury, a major breakthrough given that almost a century would pass before the appeal court came into existence.

Those who opposed the capital code were drawn from rationalists, radicals and lawyers as well as Quakers and evangelicals and they based their arguments not only on the cruelty of the punishment but also on its failure to deter. "It's viciousness corrupted the people. Because punishments were excessive, they lost the support of prosecutors and juries whose endorsement of the law was essential." [1] Ewart made a further attempt for full abolition in 1847 saying that he believed "it was necessary to give the people not a horror of the punishment but a horror of the crime – through education." [2] This time only his fellow Radicals supported him and the Home Secretary, Sir George Grey, told him that "it was impossible for the Government to inflict capital punishment against the operation of public opinion and he believed public opinion was opposed to abolition." [3] Nine years later Ewart asked for a Select Committee on the issue but, encouraged by Sir George Grey, who was again Home Secretary, the Commons refused the motion.

As soon as he was able, after Mary Timney's distressing death, William Ewart made one final attempt to achieve his long held

William Ewart Member of Parliament for Dumfries at the time of Mary's trial and execution.

ambition of abolishing the death sentence. In 1864 he moved "for a Select Committee to inquire into the expediency of maintaining the punishment of death" and asked his fellow MPs to once more reconsider "this vital question and inquire whether you cannot safely resign the awful attribute of disposing of human life into the hands of Him who gave it." [4]

The newspaper coverage of cases like Mary Timney's and the widespread condemnation it had received had brought about a shift in public opinion on the subject, Ewart's motion gained far more attention than it ever had before. The Home Secretary, again Ewart's adversary Sir George Grey, suggested that a Royal Commission would be better than a Select Committee and Ewart agreed. It was appointed in July 1864 and consisted of twelve members including the Duke of Richmond, Ewart, John Bright, Lord Stanley, Stephen Lushington, the Attorney General for Ireland and the Advocate for Scotland. The aim was "To inquire into the provisions and operation of the laws now in force in the United Kingdom, under and by virtue of which the punishment of death may be inflicted upon persons convicted of certain crimes and also into the manner in which capital sentences are carried into execution, and to report whether any, and if any what alteration is desirable in such laws, or any of them, or in the manner in which such sentences are carried into execution."

The Commissioners met to take evidence fifteen times over the following six months, hearing from witnesses including lawyers, chaplains, prison governors, statesmen and leaders of opinion. Some were convinced that death was the greatest deterrent, others were equally of the opinion that it was not. There were arguments on both sides that it was justified or unjustified according to religious texts. The Chaplain of Horsemonger Lane Gaol, for example, said that it was quite indefensible on religious, political and social grounds. The opinions of judges from England, Scotland and Ireland were heard and almost all were in favour of retaining the punishment.

The presentation of the report was delayed when it became clear that as a result of the consultation process the Commissioners were hopelessly divided and in a state of confusion. Ewart worked hard to convince a majority to support the abolition but in the end only three of them signed his declaration that "capital punishment might safely and with advantage to the community be at once abolished." The Attorney General for Ireland stated that he felt the weight of evidence backed Ewart's position but public opinion was not ready. The result of the whole process was compromise. They recommended that attention be paid to criminal appeals on matters of fact, to the Crown's prerogative of mercy, to the question of insanity relieving an accused person from penal responsibility and finally they recommended the abolition of public executions.

This came as an enormous disappointment to Ewart. He had always objected to any move to limit the number of witnesses, once proposed back in 1841, or create 'private' executions. He strongly believed that if public executions ended then capital punishment might continue indefinitely. Five Commissioners, including Ewart and the Lord Advocate for Scotland, declared their opposition to the ending of public executions but in 1868 a Bill was introduced to the House seeking to "permit Capital Punishment to be carried out under certain regulations within the interior of prisons." A general election held at the time meant that a government was elected that was ready to implement the recommendations of the Royal Commission. There was much support, MPs calling public executions "a disgrace not only to civilization but to our common humanity" another "barbarous and demoralising" and "not in accordance with the spirit of the age." [5] *The Daily Telegraph* stated that it was a "fragment of mediaeval barbarism." Ewart did not oppose the Bill but knew it was a devastating blow to the abolitionist cause; they had been outflanked. The minor triumph of humanitarian feeling on this small part of the issue blocked the successful progress of further attempts to do away with the punishment all together. The Society for the Abolition of Capital Punishment was suspended during the 1860s due to a lack of support and was disbanded after the report of the 1866 Royal Commission. It would later reappear as the Howard League for Penal Reform but Ewart's fears would be proved correct when the death sentence, safely hidden from public view, continued for almost a century after his death in 1869. The final executions in the United Kingdom were held in the early 1960s but some forms of capital punishment remained on the statute books until the end of the twentieth century.

Thirteen

"She was very reckless in a passion and did not care what she did or said"

There is no doubt that Mary Reid or Timney was responsible for the death of Ann Hannah but did she really deserve to be punished by public execution? It remains a matter of opinion whether this was an act of premeditated murder or culpable homicide, whether the lies she told were devious or desperate, whether she was a murderess or a victim of the state. Had Judge Deas made his decision before entering the court or did he make a fair assessment of the evidence that was before him? Mary clearly did not help herself but, as was said about Jessie McLachlan, was she a pathological liar or a panic-stricken woman in a desperate situation?

The precognition papers lying in the archives in Edinburgh give an insight into the events leading up to the murder that was not reflected in the newspaper coverage at the time. Although statements were made and information from the process leaked to the press before the trial, evidence that was favourable to Mary was not only left out of the papers but also omitted from the trial presumably because her defence advocate would have had little time to go through the statements and even less time with his client. If Mary had been allowed the rights of a modern prisoner her advocate Mr Cowan would have perhaps been able to mount a better defence, it certainly couldn't have been any worse. He could, perhaps, have drawn on Mary's impoverished and neglected upbringing and the breakdown in the relationship between the two women in the weeks before the murder. Based on archive documents and the statements given by witnesses during the precognition let's now look again at the murder of Ann Hannah and the tragedy of Mary Timney.

According to Mary's confession to the prison chaplain the Timney family had lived happily together until they moved into the tiny one room cottage at Carsphad two years before the murder. The nearby farmhouse had been the home of the Hannah's for more than forty years, Ann having shared the kitchen with her mother for most of her life and at one time her grandmother too, while her brothers slept in the second room. Three of the brothers had left the farm, though Lockhart had returned from working in Wales, without his wife, some time before 1859. In June of that year, having caused concern to his family, Lockhart was sent to Kirkcudbright to be examined before being admitted to the Southern Counties Asylum, a hospital for the poor attached to the Crichton Royal Infirmary in Dumfries, for treatment paid for by the parish of Kells.

The case book for the period notes that at the time he was a forty one year old labourer but the cause of his health difficulties was unknown.[1] He was removed on the twenty-first of November that year but from William's evidence Lockhart did not return home until March of 1860. He then came and went from Carsphad for the next few months. William admitted that his elder brother and Ann argued over a horse, the result of which was that he left home again for some months only returning in the middle of June 1861 shortly before their mother's death. After that the three siblings had lived "peaceably" together on the best of terms. William described his twin sister as having a "quiet disposition, rather nervous, she would cry if anyone spoke hastily to her but she was a good worker and generally managed everything about the house. She was never sickly but was a strong woman. She was hardy and stout. She could help me lift a sack of corn." Lockhart said she was "cheerful and good tempered, not of a melancholy disposition."

Margaret Hannah, as the holder of the tenancy for the eighteen acre farm, had leased the cottage to the Timneys and from the witness statements it appears that she had been kind to Mary, as a widowed mother of five she probably saw something of herself in the young woman's situation. Even after her death the good terms that existed between the two families appear to have continued, at least initially. William was very clear in his evidence that he knew Ann did not like Mary Timney though he said that at first she had continued the small favours started by their mother, loans of tea and sugar. Until five weeks before the murder he saw the family two or three times a week. In Mary's first statement she told William Hyacinth Dunbar, the Advocate Steward Substitute, that "up to last harvest I had been in the habit of occasionally going into the house occupied by the Hannahs and Ann Hannah was in the way of coming into ours as neighbours. She gave up doing this some time about harvest time. There was no reason for our giving up going into each other's houses at first or until lately." [2]

Mary seemed to be saying that it was Ann that stopped going into the Timney's cottage in the neighbourly way they had been used to and this is backed up by a statement made by eleven year old Benjamin Logan Barbour who had been staying with the Hannah's to help with the harvest. He told the investigation that whilst staying at Carsphad he'd visited the Timneys two or three times a week, though Frank was seldom there. "Ann Hannah told me no to go about Mary Timney as she was a bad one so I didn't go so often after this," he said. Mary's stepfather, eighty four year old Samuel Good said that his wife also hadn't been to see her daughter since harvest and had never been "in the habit of going to Carsphad and Mary Timney did not come much to our house."

As the newspapers made references to Mary's appalling upbringing and childhood it is, perhaps, not surprising that she had a difficult relationship with her mother, though it is important to remember that the press represented a middle class view of a what was a poor, peasant household. Given the fact that she tried to blame her mother for the murder of her neighbour describing their relationship as difficult is, perhaps, something of an understatement. For a young mother of four children living in poverty with only one near neighbour, the lack of support from her family must have created its own problems. It appears that although Mary hadn't seen her mother for some months, her husband Frank had. He regularly passed through Dalry on his journey to and from work and in her statement their eldest daughter Susan described how on the Saturday before the murder she had been sent to the village to meet her father. She met him at her grandmother's house. Margaret Good and Frank were, after all, a similar age and he had become a lodger at her house in Polharrow when Mary was still young. After the murder Frank and the children moved in with Mary's mother.

Although Frank Timney always described himself, in census returns, as a labourer it is unclear how long had he been working as a road surface man. What is apparent is that certainly for the final weeks of 1861 he had been working at a distance from home on the road between New Galloway and Dumfries and on the morning of the murder he'd told William Hannah that he had possibly one more week's work there. Mary Black or Clacherty told the murder investigators that Frank had been lodging for the previous month at her house in Crago, a tiny hamlet just north west of Corsock. Frank worked with her husband James on the roads in the district and only went home every alternate Saturday normally returning on Sunday. Corsock was more than fourteen miles from Carsphad, not a manageable walking distance on a daily basis for anyone let alone a man described by one witness as "lame."

As 1861 drew to a close Mary was isolated and hungry in a tiny one room cottage with four children under nine, one a baby of less than a year, with no neighbourly visits or support from her family, a husband who was largely absent and on top of that a growing suspicion that something was going on between him and the woman next door. It would be wrong, though, to portray Mary entirely as a victim. She was a woman with a reputation, a reputation that many were happy to gossip about to the press and the police. Agnes McLellan, Ann Hannah's close friend, had known Mary for many years and described her as having "a bad temper." "I have seen her in a passion. She was very reckless in a passion and did not care what she did or said," she told the investigators, adding that she had also seen her "the worse for liquor sometimes." Agnes, better known by the traditional pet name of Nan or Nanny, had often visited Ann Hannah but not Mary, though she only lived sixty yards further along the turnpike road. She had been to bake oatcakes for her once or twice after Mary had given birth to her son and after Mary's mother had returned to Dalry, but that had been a year before and she had not been to the cottage since. Nan McLellan admitted that Ann sometimes talked about Mary saying she wasn't a nice neighbour and she wanted to have somebody else in the house rented by the Timneys but she claimed that she had not spoken of any quarrels.

The police constable of New Galloway, who arrested Mary, attested that "the woman Timney holds very bad character in the country for being a drunken, ill tempered woman." He added that, like many of the witnesses, he had never heard anything against the woman Hannah describing her as "quiet and inoffensive." Elizabeth McCormick or Coates, aged fifty, who lived a quarter of a mile away at Knocknalling Lodge, emphasised that she did not associate "in any way" with Mrs Timney and claimed to know little about her though her husband, fifty seven year old Robert, a forester, said he'd known her since she was a little girl but only knew her to speak to and had "little or no acquaintance with her."

Many of the witnesses described Ann Hannah as a "quiet, inoffensive woman", the exact same words repeated in a number of statements and the evidence of Charles Patterson, the land steward for Knocknalling estate, perhaps gives some insight into what could have been happening during the interviews. According to the written statement he uses the exact same words to describe Ann Hannah and then goes on to comment "I cannot say from personal knowledge that Mrs Timney was a bad, dissipate woman but I know such is the county report of her character."

Given the number of times 'quiet and inoffensive' are used to describe Ann Hannah and 'bad and dissipate' applied to Mary Timney, it seems likely that when being questioned witnesses were being asked if they would describe the women in these terms. This would explain Charles Patterson's reply and the reason why so many statements use the same language to describe the women. The vast majority of the statements were taken down by the minister Rev Maitland and then signed by the interviewee, not hand written by the person. Most state that they can read and write but are out of practice as to their reason for not writing their own words. Inevitably, these statements are an abbreviated version of the words spoken in answer by the witnesses.

Harriet Trim, the housekeeper at Knocknalling was another who used exactly the same words in her statement adding that she had seen Mary "very drunk at Dalry" though she admitted this had been a "long time since." Like Charles Patterson she had heard of her getting into violent passions but had never actually seen her in one. Dairymaid Agnes Corrie, who had known both Mary and Ann for three years, also said she had never seen her "worse of liquor" but she had obviously been asked the question. Interestingly, Mary's step sister Jane Good also said she had heard of her "frequently being in liquor but I never saw her so, I have seen her sister often drunk however." Dalry innkeeper William Glendenning, however, said that on a stormy Monday at the end of November Mary had wanted to sit at the fireside to wait for her husband who had been to Castle Douglas for his pay and was expected on the omnibus. "She was not sober," he said.

It is entirely possible that these descriptions of the two women, almost depicting one as a saint and the other a sinner, were quite true, but a fuller picture of their characters was not ascertained due to the leading nature of the questioning. Much of Mary's reputation as a drunken, volatile, spendthrift may have, to some degree, been derived from tittle tattle. Ann Hannah may indeed have been a quiet and inoffensive woman but there was clearly more to her personality than the meek temperament described by her brothers and friends. Mary Timney certainly saw a different side to her neighbour in the final weeks of 1861 but it is impossible to know what brought about this change in Ann's attitude towards the younger woman, if it was a change. Ann may have nursed a dislike for her young neighbour for years but it had remained hidden while her mother, who clearly had some compassion for Mary, was alive.

There was speculation in the community after the murder about a relationship between Frank and Ann. Mary told the prison chaplain of her feelings of jealousy but Ann may simply have realised that as she had gained control of the household following her mother's death, she could finally give vent to her dislike of the woman. It appears that the difficulties began when the two women stopped visiting each other's homes in the neighbourly way they had been used to, though this change did not seem to effect the men. Lockhart continued to visit the Timneys on a regular basis and William said that he saw them two or three times a week until the women's quarrel. Mary also claimed that Frank was in the habit of going to sit with Ann Hannah when her brothers were away. It was during one of these friendly visits that Lockhart witnessed Mary's temper for himself. He told the investigation that "Frank Timney often told me he had a horrid life with her, that she wasted everything and that he could not trust her with a shilling and she behaved badly in every way to him." He said that about a month before he'd seen Frank go passed their door "very wet and ill looking." At Ann's suggestion Lockhart had gone to see how he was, finding him in bed with a "bad eye, bad altogether." He saw Mary arrive back at the cottage, and after some words, pick up a stool from next to the fire and throw it at her husband.

Frank appears to have played a part in what was the first flashpoint between the two women after weeks of growing tension. On his way to work one morning in December, about five weeks before the murder, Frank noticed an ash tree had been washed up by the river onto the meadow that lay on the opposite side of the road to Carsphad. He returned to the cottage to tell Mary to take a barrow down and collect some of the wood. Gathering sticks was a major occupation for Mary and the older daughters as this would have been the cheapest way to heat the cottage although they did use some coal which was available in the district, brought down by cart from the mines in Ayrshire. According to William there had been a quarrel two or three days earlier between the two women.

Mary had placed some branches of the tree into the barrow and was wheeling it along the road past the farmhouse when she was stopped by Ann Hannah who had been watching her from her doorway. Mary claimed the older woman said that the wood belonged to the farm and then accused her of thieving not only the sticks but also some turnips. Ann Hannah threatened to put a stop to her by reporting her to the estate's forester, Mr Brown. William said his sister had told him she'd said "Mary, you are at the old work again but we'll put a stop to it." She'd reported that Mary had replied that as it was water wreck it was free to anybody but she had told her it wasn't water wreck and she had no right to it. The Hannah brothers said that Ann told them there had been a lot of bad language from Mary and the young woman had lifted a stone and threatened her with it, but Ann had just laughed at her. Ann was a much bigger, stronger woman and Lockhart stated that his sister had said she "was not the least afraid of Mary". In his evidence at the trial William referred to two incidents during the same week and it's possible that Mary's threat with the stone was several days after the first argument over the wood.

The first incident was witnessed by sixty four year old Agnes Corrie who had been on her way along the turnpike road from her home in Carsphairn to visit her daughter, the dairymaid at Knocknalling. She told the investigation that the weather was stormy and there had been a flood. As she came along the road she could see Mrs Timney with her barrow of sticks arguing with Ann Hannah. She reported that she'd been frightened, and had passed by without looking up but had overheard Mary shout "You had no business coming out and attacking me on the road you great muckle yellow bitch." Mary tried to get permission to gather the sticks from James Barbour, the son of a neighbouring farmer, when he passed by the houses later that week driving some sheep but he told her he didn't have the authority.

Both women complained bitterly about each other to the men. Mary tackled William when he was working in the pig sty, a building that stood in the land between the two houses. Mary was furious insisting the wood was water wreck but William told her that if it was on their land she had no business carrying it away. "She became very high, loud and angry and I told her to keep quiet and be off for I wouldn't stand any more from her." William added that Mary had then said Ann had called her a thief and a liar. William had already heard about the incident from his sister and, as a man who liked a quiet, peaceful life, he did not appreciate 'the outburst from his fiery neighbour. Ann claimed she had done nothing to aggravate Mary but would "not allow her to do anything in the way of mischief about the place."

When Frank returned home Mary told him of Ann's threats and accusations, she was furious at being called a thief. Frank said that he never heard his wife threaten Mrs Hannah though "she was going to the police about it [the dispute] but I stopped her". William spoke to Frank in the hope of bringing an end to the episode. He promised to do what he could to keep Ann from further quarrelling but asked Frank to talk to his wife. "He told me that he dare not speak to her as she would fly at him. I said he must mildly tell her not to make these disturbances and I would speak to Ann." Frank had promised to do what he could. "I think he must have told her," William added, "as since that time I have not seen or heard of her carrying away wood or in any way annoying my sister." Ann, however, continued to lobby her brother to get rid of the Timneys and Lockhart reported that she had told Mary that "she would have her away by Whit Sunday and sooner, if possible, if she did not behave herself." About this time Ann came across the New Galloway policeman, John Robson and she asked him if "Timney's wife" had been down to see him about her as she had threatened to. Asked why, Ann told him it was because they had "had some words" and she had accused her of being a thief. The officer told her that if it was just words he would have nothing to do with it and he later said that Ann had joked about the whole thing.

Some of the evidence given by the Hannah brothers highlights the great difference between the poverty of one family and the relative prosperity of the other. The Hannahs were doing well enough in the winter of 1862 to add the tenancy of the small nearby farm at Greenloup to their fields at Carsphad. The Timneys on the other hand were a family of six dependent on any casual work Frank could find as an unskilled man in his fifties. Both the Hannah and Timney households, typically of the Glenkens, kept pigs, either for their own consumption or for fattening to sell. After the murder when Mary was asked about the money that was found in her house, she'd claimed that she'd sold a pig and not told her husband about it. This is entirely plausible as a Dalry grocer, David Cowan, told the police that the Timneys had promised to settle an outstanding bill after killing a pig, though they had failed to do this and he had refused them further credit from the December. The truth was that Mary was struggling to feed their animals. Lockhart had learned from his regular visits with Frank that he was going to sell the remaining pig as "he had not the feeding for it and had no money in the house." William suggested that they buy it but leave it in the Timney's sty as they had "plenty" and Ann could take over the care of it, it would make her a bit of money but she told her brothers that she thought Mary would poison it first.

A month before the murder when the Hannahs had been killing some of their pigs, Catherine Sherman, an eighteen year old from Dalry, had called on Mary Timney on her way to Carsphairn. According to the girl it was during this visit that Mary had claimed that when the brothers were away her man went and sat a while with Ann Hannah. Catherine would later attest in court that Mary had threatened to make Ann "a corpse one day" and was "greatly excited and in a great passion, clenching her fists as she spoke about Ann." Catherine had plenty to say about Mary and appeared to know a great deal about the Timneys saying that two days later she had warned William Hannah about Mary's threat but he'd replied that the women were always quarrelling but he didn't think they would lay hands on each other. She claimed that Frank had asked Ann to stop lending things to Mary as he was unable to repay it, and this had made Mary more angry. Catherine added that she had "often seen Mary the worse for liquor in Dalry, very drunk" and had caught her, last July after the Dalry Races, lying with a man in a field near the village who she was sure was not her husband but a stranger. When she mentioned it to her landlady Elizabeth Reid, she'd answered "oh that is nothing, I have heard of Mary being often with other men." Interestingly, Catherine's statement about Mary threatening to leave Ann "a corpse one day" was quoted in *The Scotsman* in the days after the murder, the source presumably being *The Dumfries Courier*'s 'man on the spot,' but the newspaper had commented that "story is not quite credible but we give it as we have heard it."

Catherine, credible or not, was not the only person to mention Mary being seen with other men. Nan McLellan had gone to Carsphad on the Thursday before the murder, to watch over Ann's house while her friend went to Dalry to buy, among other things, tea and sugar. On her return the two women had chatted and Mary featured in the conversation. Ann told her friend she had seen a man called Clugston pass by her house going up the road, and then saw him go into the woods with Mrs Timney. "She did not say what for but I understood her to mean it was for no good purpose," Nan McLellan said. When questioned during the investigation, Mary's eldest daughter Susan admitted that the man Clugston had called at the house that day asking for her mother who was in the woods collecting sticks. Susan described how he had returned with her mother to the cottage and she had been asked to take all the children out to play.

By the winter of 1861, for whatever reason, Mary and Frank were not living happily together. In conversations with his neighbours Frank blamed Mary for their miserable life, citing her bad temper and her inability to handle the little money he earned, though William in his letter to the papers made it clear he believed it was enough for them to live on. Yet witness after witness also told of how Mary had been reduced to asking to borrow money or a "wee pickle tea." Dairymaid Agnes Corrie said that when Mary called again at Knocknallling she knew that she had been refused "two or three times" before. Mary had asked to speak to the housekeeper but Agnes refused to fetch her. James Richardson, the constable from Carsphairn said that he was passing one day before Ann Hannah's death and Mary had asked to borrow sixpence but he'd told her to get it from the Hannahs. She'd replied that she would not go there. John McAdam, a servant employed by John Lawson Kennedy of Knocknalling, said Mary had often asked if she could borrow some tea but not for some time before the attack.

Not everyone rebuffed her requests though. Even those living nearby on the Knocknalling estate gave milk to the children who called down most days to collect it. Forty eight year old Mary Barbour, who was married to the toll keeper and lived two miles further along the turnpike road, was the mother of two of the crucial witnesses, but she spoke kindly of Mary Timney though that part of her evidence was never shared with the jury. The two girls, Jane, ten and seven year old Margaret were in the habit of going into the Timney's cottage on their way to school. "She was always very kind to them, allowing them to warm themselves," she said. She knew Mary to speak to and had occasionally called in herself as she passed the cottage on the way to church. Mary Barbour said she was "not particularly acquainted with Ann Hannah" though on the last Sunday of the year she had been briefly in the farmhouse at Carsphad. With the sound of the Timney's swine squealing in the background "she

[Ann] said it's a pity about the swine, meaning they were neglected. I said it was a greater pity about the children as I thought they were neglected in their education. That was all that passed," Mary said in her statement. Mary Barbour clearly believed that Ann Hannah cared more about the hungry pigs than the hungry Timney children. Mary Barbour, however, was happy to lend the odd item to the young mother. "I lent them because she was kind to my children, it was not often," she told the investigation, "sometimes she sent her own children, sometimes I sent my girls to take what she wanted to her, she never borrowed anything from me herself."

But from Mary Barbour's evidence it was clear that things were getting worse for the Timney family. The eldest girl, Susan was sent for "a loan of meal" but Mary was only able to give her a little as she hadn't much in the house. Three days later Susan appeared again to ask to borrow ten pence or a shilling. "I did not lend her any money but I asked the girl if she was hungry and she said she had nothing to eat. I took off her pinafore and gave her a fill of meal. I also gave her a little tea, though she had not asked for it." Mary Barbour appears to have been one of the few people amongst Mary Timney's neighbours who had compassion for the young woman, she said that she had never had a conversation about Ann Hannah with her or heard tales about her. None of this evidence was brought out in court.

Fourteen

"I lifted my sister in my arms and spoke to her but she never recognised me."

The end of the year came and went, though the thirteenth of January, the day of the murder was the first day of the old Scots calender. There would have been little to celebrate in the Timney house with four young children to care for, perhaps another period without work ahead, little feed for the pig and no money in the house. Frank met his daughter Susan in Dalry at her grandmother's house on Saturday the eleventh of January. Mary would later claim that she had sent Susan to buy tea and sugar at William Smith's grocers but all the shopkeepers in the village denied seeing the girl that day. Susan told the police that she had not been given money to buy anything. Father and daughter had returned to Carsphad together in the afternoon.[1]

On the Sunday night Lockhart visited the Timneys and recalled being asked by Mary what they'd been doing recently and if he and William would be going to Greenloup, the land they'd recently acquired, on the following morning. Both Frank and Lockhart, amongst many others, later verified that Mary was wearing her green tartan dress, the same dress she would say she hadn't worn for weeks. The next day, Monday the thirteenth of January started early for the inhabitants of both households. Frank had already left by the time Susan got up. Her father usually left on the Sunday evening but he had waited until the Monday morning to borrow half a crown from William Hannah. The Hannahs had also risen early, at six o'clock, William lighting the candle before going out to thresh in the barn. Ann began to prepare the breakfast. William cleaned the stable and gave meal to the cows and the horse. It was when he was cleaning the byre at seven o'clock that Frank Timney, who had made his own breakfast of porridge and milk, appeared asking for a loan. "William, could I trouble you to lend me two shillings till the end of the week as there is nothing in the house," he said. William told the police that Frank had promised to repay the money on the Saturday along with what he owed for a cart of coal and its transport. "I had no silver but half a crown which I gave him. He said he would leave it with his wife so she could get something for the children as there was nothing for them." Frank left for work and three quarters of an hour later William saw Mary at their sty feeding the pig. At eight o'clock the three siblings breakfasted together before William and his brother left for the fields at Greenloup taking the horse and cart with them to carry stones. Ann was still eating when they left. They began work at ten o'clock, William repairing the dykes and Lockhart cutting new drains, they were never more than ten minutes walk from each other.

In the Timney house Susan and Mary shared a little tea and oatmeal cake. There were some farls left, that would be taken away as evidence by the police, that Susan later placed in the press under some clothes. The oatcakes had been baked by her mother on Saturday according to Susan but she wanted them hidden when she asked the girl to fetch Nanny McLellan. It's clear from this that Mary did not need any baking done, the message was an excuse for Susan to get Nan to come to Carsphad as Mary must have known that she would call at the farmhouse and find Ann. Frank Timney, meanwhile, was on his way to work. He was seen by innkeeper William Glendenning passing through Dalry at nine o'clock. He told the investigation that it would "take an hour to walk from Dalry to the twenty-two mile stone on the Dumfries road at Balmaclellan and the same time to walk from here to Carsphad. As Timney is lame it would take him longer to get to either place." John Fergusson, a sixty year old labourer, said he'd met Frank at the twenty two mile stone between ten and eleven o'clock. Corsock was a further two hours walking from there. Samuel Clacherty, also sixty and a road surfaceman knew Frank as he was working and lodging with his son James. He told the police that he knew what time it was as the drainers working nearby always took their dinner at noon and that was about an hour after Frank had gone by.

At twenty five minutes before ten o'clock Mary Barbour's two girls along with their friend twelve year old Agnes Sproat were passing by the two houses at Carsphad on the way to school at Polharrow. The school had been built in 1842 by John Kennedy of Knocknalling in remembrance of his daughter Marianne Ewart Kennedy. It had books, drawing cards and a folding bed in case the teacher was storm bound. The two Barbour girls went into the Timney cottage as they often did, Mary was cleaning something with a cloth they told the police. Agnes spoke to Susan who said they were not going to school that day. The girls also saw Ann Hannah standing at her door, when Agnes asked the time she'd assured them they were not late; school started at ten o'clock. Agnes lived with her grandfather at Strangassel farm, further along from the Barbours, and Ann talked to the girl about ploughing. "If it was dry enough to plough Willie would do it" Ann had said but if it was not dry enough she would send for the beast belonging to Agnes's grandfather. Ann asked Agnes to call in on her way home from school so that she could tell her what she'd decided about the ploughing. All the girls remembered Mary in her tartan dress and Ann in her distinctive scarlet and red 'prudence cap.'

Not long after the girls had passed by Mary left the house and was gone for about half an hour. There is only Mary's final confession to the prison chaplain to give any clue as to what happened in that farmhouse kitchen. Susan told the police that she went to sit by the fire but had then gone to the door where she saw her mother leave the farmhouse and come straight home. "I saw in her hand a wooden beetle which I know belonged to my mother," Susan said clearly in her statement adding that the three girls used to "make a doll" of the implement. Mary had been wearing her tartan dress over the top of her bedgown, the sleeves of the dress were shorter than the gown and Susan saw that one was covered in blood and there was blood on the frock itself. As Mary washed blood from her neck she told her daughter that she had "near killed Ann. She had knocked her down on the floor with the beetle and kicked and knocked her."

On Susan's signed statement in the precognition papers there is a note saying "the girl is sharp and intelligent for her years and spoke without contradiction or hesitation." However, there is a statement in the archive at Broughton House in Kirkcudbright that differs slightly from the one included in the precognition papers. The archive also has a statement from Frank Timney and although the file refers to the Castle Douglas solicitor, Richard Hewatt who as an agent for the poor had been allocated to the case on Mary's behalf, setting out in a close carriage and pair to take the documents to be included in the precognition, they are not in the Edinburgh collection. There are no statements from Frank or Margaret Corson. In the Kirkcudbright archive statement she says she saw her mother go into Carsphad farmhouse but when she left the cottage "she had no a batt in her hand nor anything else I saw."[2]

She also says that she and the other children "the bairn, Maggy and Mary" had gone "a bit down the brae" when her mother came out of the farmhouse and they had all returned home. In this statement Susan confirmed that her mother had the 'batt' in her hand on coming out of the farmhouse, the implement "belonged to us, I think it was ours as we had one like it." Susan saw her mother wash the beetle and dry it with a cloth. Susan's sister Margaret, described, as "intelligent but frightened" explained that their father had told the older girls not to go to school that day. She too had seen the blood on her mother's sleeve and saw her wash the beetle in a small tub.

Mary had carried out a brutal attack on her neighbour and had, possibly, carried the beetle with her but that does not prove that she had gone with intent to kill. In fact further evidence from her daughter Susan casts doubt on Lord Deas conviction that she had. In the statement to Mr Hewat Susan states that her mother had not said that she had nearly killed Ann Hannah but just that she'd battered her and left her bleeding. Before taking to her bed and asking her daughter to fetch Nan McLellan Mary had gone down again to the farmhouse "to see if Ann was still lying on the floor." Mary obviously knew she had left Ann badly hurt but she clearly thought that she was not so severely injured that she wouldn't begin to recover shortly afterwards. A little while later Mary asked Susan to go down to the farmhouse to see if Ann "had yet risen from the floor." The child reluctantly went and looked through the kitchen window and there saw Ann Hannah "lying all bloody on the floor." Mary went to bed then complaining of her head but sent Susan to fetch Nanny McLellan to ask her to bake surely knowing that the woman would call in on her friend and discover what had happened. Susan did not say anything about what she had seen to Nanny "or anybody else as mother had told me not to tell anybody."

Though Mary would continue to deny the beetle had been hers, Susan was clear in her first statement that the implement belonged to them and had never been loaned to Ann Hannah or been away from their cottage. After she'd returned from Polharrow Bridge, where Nan McLellan lived, Susan was asked by her mother to keep a watch. About an hour later she saw Nan go into the farmhouse briefly before running off. Mary bundled up the clothes she'd attempted to wash and put them in the loft above the beds. Nan had approached the farmhouse meaning to call in on her friend but had noticed that the outer door was open and the kitchen door to the left, was a little ajar. "I heard the cows lowing in the byre as if they hadn't been attended to," she said. Pushing open the door she saw Ann, without her distinctive knitted prudence cap, lying in the middle of the kitchen, "her hair was wet with blood, she was in such a mess. The floor and all about seemed covered in blood." She ran off to alert Elizabeth Coates at Knocknallling Lodge, not to Mary Timney's because she "believed she was lying and besides she was not a woman that one would have gone to for any help."

Nan returned with Mrs Coates, John McAdam, who had been home having lunch, and not far behind them, Robert Coates. All four looked carefully at everything in the kitchen before they touched anything. They saw a bloodstained knife and a poker by Ann's right hand. Nan described the scene: "the floor was unevenly paved and the blood had run into the crevices. On the opposite side from the door and the window, [near the dresser Robert Coates added] there was a mark of a hand as if a cloth had been dragged along but there was no sign of a struggle, the chairs were not upset. There was a small tub upside down and the clothes she had been wringing were partly under the tub and partly under her head." It was clear that Ann had been washing at the table by the window there was a larger tub with water that had been "blued."

It was obvious to them all that Ann was very badly injured, her distinctive winter prudence cap was blood soaked and there was a large wound to the back of the head, Robert Coates had immediately checked to see if her throat had been cut. Nan McLellan described how blood had run all down Ann's shoulders, inside her shift and her stays were stained with blood. From this it would seem that, unlike the graphic scenarios invented by the press, Ann had not been immediately felled from behind by a sudden, unexpected blow. If that had been the case the blood would not have flowed into her clothing in the way described by her friend. For the blood to flow down her shoulders and into her undergarments Ann must have remained on her feet long enough for this to have happened which would fit more with Mary's version of events, that there been in a violent struggle between the two women. William's statement also points towards a fight with Ann probably grabbing the nearest weapons to hand, the knife on the dresser and the poker at the fire. "My sister would never let anyone get across to the fireplace to use this poker as it was on the opposite side from the door where anyone would come in. My sister always washed at the table before the window in the kitchen, she had washed on Friday and dried shirts for my brother and me on Saturday but she was bluing some white clothing in preparation to hang them out to dry." The ordered furniture and the mark of a cloth having been dragged along on the floor surely indicated that someone had attempted to clear up after the struggle, not that a struggle had never taken place.

Susan appeared at the farmhouse door holding the baby asking "What's ado Nanny?" Nan replied that Ann Hannah was nearly killed and at this Susan ran home. Mary arrived soon after, commenting that "this is an unco job" to which Nan replied "Yes, it is a dreadful, dreadful affair." All the neighbours said that Mary was not in any way agitated and appeared "quite cool and collected." They all questioned her, asking had she not seen anything on the road to which she'd answered no, she'd been in her bed poorly.

Out in the fields at Greenloup the two Hannah brothers had loosed the horse and sat down to have their dinner at about one o'clock. Afterwards they went to look at the drains that Lockhart had been cutting when a woman called Mary Duff found them. She told William that he must "go home fast" for his sister was very bad, she didn't know what was the matter just that she'd been taken ill suddenly. William's first thought was colic. He told his brother to work on a bit and then return home with the horse and cart but Mrs Duff said she thought they should both go. "I told Lockhart to bring the horse and cart by the road, I would cross the fields. I then ran home and on the road met Robert Coates," William said. Robert told him not to be alarmed but William knew something serious had happened as the man was crying and he could see a lot of women standing at the farmhouse door. "I went in but was so agitated I cannot tell who was there. I lifted my sister in my arms and spoke to her but she never recognised me," William explained. He checked the house to see if anything had been taken, finding his key and the chest where he kept his money, it was all there "it was not done for plunder" he concluded, however later he would note the loss of two purses, though one was later found, and tea missing from the cannister. "My sister was very particular about things. I found the empty cannister with the lid turned upside down, she would never have left it as I found it. I knew she'd bought tea and sugar on the previous Thursday." Before leaving to find Lockhart and send him to alert the police in New Galloway he told Mary, who was sitting at the fire with her fretful baby, to go home as she was doing no good sitting there. She replied: "Oh indeed I may go home, I can do no good here." He'd decided to send for the police as he had suspicions against Mary as "the neighbours were talking about her at the door." As William returned with the horse and cart after speaking to Lockhart he met Dr Andrew Jackson as he arrived and confided "I suspect there has been foul play." The doctor asked by whom, but William said he would not mention any names.

The doctor had been alerted by the Coates' son who'd told him that "Ann Hannah had got herself hurt and was lying in blood." He'd packed some adhesive plaster and things necessary for dressing wounds and driven to Carsphad immediately arriving at twenty minutes past two. Ann was "quite senseless," the knitted cap and both shoulders of her dress were saturated in blood, "her pulse was scarcely perceptible, her whole body was collapsed and the extremities cold, her breathing was slow and laborious." Dr Jackson washed and dressed Ann's wounds, gave her some wine and applied warm water to her hands and feet and did what he could to bring her round but without effect. After several hours he was joined by Dr Millman, who had also brought his student son with him. The doctor had been shown the knife and the poker but did not believe that either of the weapons could have produced the wounds to the head.

At around four o'clock little Margaret Timney arrived at Knocknalling House to fetch milk. Housekeeper Harriet Trim told the investigators that the family regularly got milk from the house. Mrs Trim had been up at the farmhouse earlier in the afternoon and knew all about "the murder." She asked the child if she knew how Ann Hannah was and the girl had replied that she was dead, and began crying. The housekeeper had then asked if her mother had been to the farmhouse in the morning and she'd answered yes for a "wee while", at about ten o'clock. Some time before five o'clock thirty two year old police constable John Robson was met by his children who told him he was wanted back in New Galloway where he found Lockhart. He immediately engaged the omnibus – referred to as the 'machine' by Lockhart in his statement – and alerted Dr Millman who travelled ahead of him. On his arrival the constable noticed that the floor of the room had been washed. He went and "spoke loudly to Ann Hannah but she paid no attention," he said in his statement. Although the victim was unable to respond the people clustered in the small kitchen had plenty to say on her behalf and from what PC Robson "heard in the house, suspicion pointed to Mary Reid or Timney." He immediately left to walk the fifty nine yards north to the Timney's cottage, taking with him Dr Millman's student son and the omnibus driver, forty five year old Robert Haugh.

Several witness statements help to give a real insight into the living conditions of the Timneys and the circumstances of the first search by the police constable. Seventeen year old William Hockin McKinley Millman said the house was "full of smoke" and there was an area to the side of the beds obviously used for storage as there were turnips, old pots and straw there. Robson admitted that the house was "very smoky and dark" whilst his colleague, William Donaldson, from Dalbeattie who took part in the search two days later commented then that the cottage had one window and open joists apart from an area of boarding above the beds. "It was very bare of furnishings, they were very poor, the beds made of common ticking filled with chaff, though the sheets were clean."

PC Robson immediately began questioning Mary, who he'd found in her bed with her children. She said she hadn't seen any strangers, and didn't know anything about the attack on Ann. PC Robson made her get up in order to see the clothes she was wearing and he "examined her to see if there were any marks of blood. She had no marks of violence on her face or arms. She said I might look at her legs and all if I liked. There was not a mark or a scratch on her." Mary was wearing a brown polka jacket and a blue flannel petticoat shift which had spots that he "suspected to be blood." Robert Haugh said she'd taken new clothes from a chest, but the stains could have been from "soot or rain drops."

The constable searched the room, Mary complaining that he was using the only candle she had to last her until Saturday. He came across the wooden beetle behind a meal barrel but replaced it. He found tea and sugar in a drawer, which Mary claimed to be hers, a teaspoon of tea in a tin on the dresser, seven shillings and seven pence and a quantity of oatcake. The constable later stated, "I said 'odd place to have it under good clothes.'" Of course the oatcakes were not stolen from the farmhouse, simply hidden from Nan McLellan in case she had arrived at the cottage after the request to bake.

Mary told them that there was nothing in the loft but, despite the darkness, smoke and the light of a solitary candle, the young Millman thought he saw something and called Robson's attention to it. The constable then found the bundle of clothes after standing on the meal barrel and pulling himself up into the rafters. Examining the items he was immediately convinced they were marked with blood despite being recently washed. Mary claimed she hadn't worn them for three weeks since her "courses." Leaving the cottage under watch he took the confiscated items back to Carsphad to show Dr Millman, and the Hannahs in the hope they would be identified as belonging to Ann but none were recognised. After the men had left, Mary asked Susan to move the beetle from behind the barrel to under the dresser which the girl did very reluctantly. "I saw it done but did not want to do it," she told the investigators.

At the farmhouse, Ann Hannah continued to decline. Lockhart was sent by the doctor to Knocknalling to fetch some brandy but by the time he returned his sister had died. A little earlier PC Robson had gone back to the tiny cottage along with William Millman and found the door bolted. The children opened the door, Mary was sitting by the fireside and she immediately asked for the return of her clothes and the tea. The officer said he would be back to see her again before he left. She asked after Ann Hannah, enquiring if she had spoken yet, adding "I hope to God I will see Ann Hannah sitting at the fireside tomorrow night and she'll be able to tell who has done it." The constable returned to the farmhouse and on discovering that Ann had died during his absence, he arranged for the omnibus to be prepared, put all the evidence, now labelled, into a bag and went back to arrest Mary Timney.

"I said I am sorry to have to apprehend you for the wilful murder of Ann Hannah. She said she was innocent and would never have done that and if I have to answer for it in this world I'll not have to do it in the next for no person saw me doing it," PC Robson told the investigation. Mary evidently then asked how Ann was and was visibly shocked when told that she was dead. "'Dead!' she said apparently surprised," the constable reported. William Millman confirmed this: "She seemed astonished to hear that Ann Hannah was dead. She was paler after she heard of the death, nearly as white as a sheet but she kept up the same bold demeanour."

Mary, holding her baby, was then taken and placed, along with daughters Susan and Mary in the omnibus with Robert Haugh while the police officer and William Millman took seven year old Margaret with them in Dr Millman's gig. The child was questioned as they travelled towards Dalry the young student later reporting that the girl had at first said that her mother had gone to Carsphad in the morning but then corrected herself and said she had not. In the omnibus Mary continued to protest her innocence admitting she had quarrelled with Ann Hannah but saying she "wished the Lord would strike her dead if she had lifted a hand to Ann." She then began to sob fearing that she would never see her children again, though Haugh assured her that if she was innocent she would see them again in a short time. She asked him if she would have to go to Kirkcudbright, little realising that this journey would eventually take her on to Dumfries to die before a crowd on the gallows.

The buildings that remain at Carsphad are the byres once belonging to the farm. The farmhouse and cottage now lie under the modern road that passes through the glen.

Fifteen

A Paroxym of Fury

The story of Mary Reid or Timney leaves many unanswered questions. *The Dumfries Courier* put it succinctly "whether this murder was a long premeditated act or the result of a sudden quarrel; whether when Mary Timney proceeded to the house of her victim she did so with the intention of committing murder or of inflicting a severe beating can never be known with certainty on this side of time."

Information contained in the precognition but not revealed in court does point towards Mary's intention being to confront her neighbour but not to kill her. She was not only denied a fair hearing but also summarily dismissed by the men around her. Frank stopped her from going to the police about the accusations Ann had made and it is impossible not to wonder if the attack could have been prevented if Mary had been allowed to have her say. William treated her complaints in a high handed and dismissive fashion whilst Ann had mocked Mary's attempt to threaten her with a stone. Police officer John Robson had been uninterested in news of Mary's complaints against Ann, and noted that Ann had joked about the incidents.

The Dumfries Standard argued that Mary's actions did not make sense if she had really been intent on murdering Ann. "Strange to say, the person who first discovered the deceased had been sent for by the convict Timney to come and bake for her that day; and but for this circumstance the crime would probably not have been discovered till the evening when the brothers of the deceased who lived with her, came home from their work and by that time all silent evidence of the convict's guilt might have been destroyed. This in itself favours the idea that the murder was not premeditated or deliberately intended but committed in a paroxysm of fury."

In the introduction to her book *Women Who Kill*,[1] Ann Jones quotes a prison warden who knew many women who had committed murder and described them as "just average, every-day sort of women" who took desperate measures in situations that most women somehow manage to cope with in more peaceable ways from day to day. "Murder is often situational," Ann Jones wrote, "given the same set of circumstances, any one of us might kill."

The Hannah twins were clearly people of principle and exacting standards, regular church goers who lived an ordered life. William described Ann as being 'very particular about things' knowing that someone had tampered with the tea because she would never have left the tin that way. The argument that led to Lockhart leaving home also hints at Ann being rather more than a "quiet and inoffensive" woman. Unmarried and childless Ann had clearly run out of sympathy for Mary, that is if she had ever had any compassion for her at all. Mary Barbour's statement implies that Ann had more concern for the welfare of Mary's pigs than for the children. Though William, to his great credit, wrote to the newspapers in favour of the campaign to save Mary from the noose he mentioned in his letter that he did not believe the Timneys were living in poverty. "Neither was she so miserably poor as mentioned, for her husband was getting thirteen shillings per week for his work" he wrote in his letter. But as a casual labourer Frank was not in continuous work and thirteen shillings would not go far.

A report carried in *The Dumfries Standard* later in 1862 highlighted the cases of three women living near Manchester, each trying to live on two shillings a week. It detailed their outgoings on flour, treacle, coffee, sugar, and bacon – the limited budget did not include tea. The article pointed out that there was no money for clothing and on this economy these young women were "verging on starvation." The Timneys were a family of six trying to live on thirteen shillings a week, when Frank could earn it, in a remote rural area where prices would have been much higher.

One of the main questions that begs an answer is why was Mary jealous and was there any truth to her belief that Ann had an influence over Frank? If Ann had developed some kind of relationship with Frank it must have been after her mother's death in June. Mary claimed that he'd taken to going in to sit with her neighbour when her brothers were away so this must have been during a period when Frank wasn't in regular work, most likely after harvest and before he found employment as a road surface man which began in November at the very latest. The statement attributed by Mary to her mother in her ridiculous allegation about the attack, "Mary I have a mind before I leave this world to give Ann Hannah her licks for setting your man against you when you were taken to Kirkcudbright" must surely be at the real heart of things. But what does it refer to? Nothing in the precognition statements or the newspaper coverage even hints at what lies behind this comment. The only clue to anything going on between Frank and his neighbour lies in two poems written about the Carsphad or Glenkens murder. One poem claims to have been written locally at the time of the trial and execution and the other, though penned seventy years after the events, was also based on local knowledge of the case.

The Carsphad Tragedy was written by Alexander Wilson who was born in Dalry on the thirteenth of January 1883 and whose grandfather had worked as an agricultural labourer on Greenloup farm.[2] In both poems Frank is described in very different terms to the way he was seen by William and Lockhart but more in line with the way he was alluded to in newspaper reports. Mr Wilson's poem describes Frank as "a bigot, drunken wretch" who married Mary when she was just seventeen and who "should [have] been drowned in Ken's dark flood" due to the dreadful life he'd caused her. The poem refers to Frank as a violent man who "instead of love" gave "blows, coarse oaths and taunting jeers" leaving Mary and the children hungry and cold. The description of Frank as a 'bigot', raises yet another seemingly unanswerable question but the author may have meant bigamist and, if so, there is a hint of an answer in the documents about the Glenkens murder held at the Carsphairn Heritage Centre. In between newspaper cuttings there is a line referring to an entry in the parish records for Dalry. Following this lead it transpires that a baptism was first registered in 1843 under the name of Thomson but this was later scored out and the name Timny or Timony written instead. It is the record of a baptism for an illegitimate child called Margaret born on the eighteenth of October 1843 and baptised on the seventh of April 1844 to parents Francis Timony and Mary Hyslop.

In 1851 unmarried Mary Hyslop, a thirty four year old farm servant from a local family, gave birth to a second illegitimate girl though this time there was no baptism recorded. It is impossible to state categorically that the father of Mary Hyslop's baby was the same Frank Timney that married Mary Reid but a search of the census records shows that the name, whatever the spelling, was uncommon with only a handful of men bearing it in the whole of Scotland at that time. Given that Frank was more than twenty years older than his wife it would not be unreasonable to believe that he may have fathered at least one child during a relationship with Mary Hyslop, a relationship that she may have considered to be an irregular marriage.

The earlier poem, which claimed to be a contemporary account, went further in its sympathies towards Mary saying that "if Ann had been decent and walked the richt way, they might both have been living at this very day." The poet refers in his rhyme to an outing when Frank and Ann "gaed awa' tae the toon" leaving Mary and the children with little fuel or food in the house while they were "sitting happy and drinking their gill, nae doubt but it laid a foundation for ill." This poem which was still known and recited by people in Dalry until the end of the twentieth century refers also to a 'wee wooden mell,' and although this description may have more to do with the poet needing to find words that rhymed it is also a reminder that unfortunately the wooden mallet was never described in detail. The children said that they used the beetle, an implement that Mary used to mash turnips, as a doll but that is the only clue to its possible size and shape. When Dumfries Museum held an exhibition about the Mary Timney case in the late 1990s some information came to light that the actual weapon from the case was still in the region but it has been impossible to confirm this. The question of the relationship between Ann Hannah and Frank Timney, along with the size of the wooden beetle or mallet, remains unanswered.

One aspect of the case that is beyond dispute, and was even accepted by the newspapers that were steadfastly unsympathetic, was Mary's devotion to her children. Even *The Glasgow Daily Herald* reported that "of her children she spoke very frequently and in a very touching manner." Her last strangled cries cut short by the gallow's drop, were for the welfare of "her weans." What happened to them, at least in terms of their immediate future, is one question that can be answered. Following the execution there was great public interest in doing something to help Mary's children. Given the references in the press to the unhappy life she'd had at the hands of her mother and then her husband it was clear that these two people would not be allowed to keep the three girls and their baby brother. An appeal, initiated in the Glenkens and administered by the Rev James Maitland, was published for people to contribute to a fund to support their education.

In the July the newspapers reported that, as a result of the appeal, arrangements had been made for all the children that would hopefully allow them to make a new start. A philanthropic woman from Bristol, having read of the case, had offered a place for the eldest girl Susan. The three remaining children were to be given new names so that their lives would not be overshadowed by their mother's fate and they would be sent to school outside the area. However, it was only the spelling of their names that was actually changed from Timney to Tymney, a somewhat ironic gesture given that their father's name had gone through numerous changes of spelling already and most people would have known of the case by word of mouth. It was, though, obviously done with good intent. The three children were sent to a newly opened industrial school in the small town of Newton Stewart, some fifty miles west of Dumfries.

As the case had been reported nationally and only the spelling of their names was changed, this move was hardly the fresh start one might have imagined they would be given. Surprisingly, the children were kept together despite being moved to the Penninghame Industrial School for Girls. These, sometimes called Ragged, schools were usually supported

A photograph of Mary's children Margaret, Mary and John taken at a studio in Newton Stewart when they were attending the Penninghame Industrial School for Girls.

by voluntary contributions to provide an education for destitute or orphaned children. The Tymney children, with John the only boy among more than twenty five girls, appear in the 1871 census record for the school which was housed in a building, now a private home, later called Windsor Lodge. Unfortunately the records for the school are unavailable, possibly lost, but there are references to the school being "homelike where each girl spent a month per year at the seaside through the offices of friends of the institution and of which the inspector declared 'I have nowhere seen girls looking better'." [3] The children at Penninghame were given an education and trained for work and were usually released into service. Unfortunately after Newton Stewart the younger children's lives become more difficult to trace.

Susan's future was easier to track as her name remained unchanged. In 1871, aged nineteen, Susan was working as a household assistant at Red Lodge Reformatory in the St Augustine district of Bristol. The institution was founded in 1854 by an educational and social reformer called Mary Carpenter following the publication of her book *Reformatory Schools for the Children of the Perishing and Dangerous Classes and for Juvenile Offenders*. It is more than likely that Miss Carpenter was the philanthropic woman referred to by the newspapers. By 1881 Susan had married printer's lithograph reader, Norwegian born Nicolas Grove and become the mother of a daughter called Ellen, who was then two years old. By the time of the 1901 census Susan's husband had died but she had trained as a proof reader whilst her twenty one year old daughter was then working as an assistant in a china shop.

In the Glenkens, William Hannah continued to live at Carsphad Farm with Nan McLellan becoming his housekeeper. It appears that his brother Lockhart's life continued to be unsettled. His mental health suffered a relapse the year following the murder when he was living and working in the parish of Tongland outside Kirkcudbright as a field labourer. Again paid for by the parish he spent a month at the Southern Counties Asylum and although he returned home he was readmitted ten years later. The records feature a lengthy medical report by Dr Alfred Millman who stated that Lockhart believed he was the owner of Carsphad farm and made threatening gestures at times though he had not "offered any violence." Both William and Nan considered him "far wrong in his mind." Lockhart never again left the asylum, living there until his death in 1878 aged sixty. The annual assessments of his condition described him as "easily offended", "irritable", with a "threatening, angry attitude." There is no mention of his sister's murder or the tragic circumstances that involved Lockhart.

It is difficult to say categorically what happened to Frank Timney. There was a Francis Timmony living in Dalry in 1871 in a house next door to Susan Reed, possibly Mary's sister, and her shoemaker husband John, but he gives his age as seventy five. In the census he describes himself as a widower originally from Ireland and working as a labourer so there is a chance it's the same man. The rarity of the name, even in its many spellings, makes it likely that this is Mary's husband and he has either simply lost track of his age or given that he married Mary when she was still in her teens, he may have then claimed to be younger then than he really was.

The final whereabouts of Mary Timney is also a mystery. Following the execution her body was buried in the precincts of the prison in Dumfries but twenty years later a new prison was built and the old building was sold. Unfortunately the authorities, the regional council and the prison service, have no record of what happened to those people that had been interred at the Buccleuch Street site. One would have imagined that the bodies were removed when the building was sold but reports in the local papers indicate that this was not the case, at least initially.

In October 1883 a public sale was held in the billiard room of the King's Arms Hotel in Dumfries and one of the lots was the old prison. A sum of £1900 was offered by John Henderson, a solicitor acting on behalf of the Mechanics Institute who proposed to erect a new hall and

The remains of Polharrow school

reading room at the site but only six months later the building was for sale again. Three years passed before the property was again mentioned in the newspapers but the article, in *The Dumfries Standard and Advertiser,* is enlightening. The old prison had remained empty but in 1886 part of the building was taken over temporarily by the police. This "afforded some of the curious an opportunity of making a closer yet voluntary acquaintance with its precincts." The reporter described the cells in the four storeys of the building as being in long straight lines with the upper tiers approached by projecting iron galleries. "There are airing courts where prisoners were allowed to walk back and forward in a short narrow passage enclosed by stone walls and barred like a cage on top. A number of these coops are built alongside of each other. With singular incongruity they have also been selected as the burial places of criminals

148

who have suffered the last penalty of the law. Opposite the grave of Mary Timney the initials MT have been rudely cut into the wall. This is in one of the female airing courts and in a portion of ground which has been reserved for the erection of a church."

It appears from this article that Mary's body was still buried at Buccleuch Street despite the fact that the prison had been sold twice for redevelopment. It can only be assumed, and hoped for, that when the old prison building was eventually demolished to make way for a proposed post office and church, Mary Timney's remains were moved and laid to rest in a grave somewhere in consecrated ground.

A pair of Victorian wooden clogs similar to those worn by Ann Hannah and Mary Timney.

This dress – made from fine woollen plaid (blue, green, black, white and yellow) – dates from 1867 and was worn as a wedding dress. It would have been of the best quality and fashion that the owner could afford and would have been beyond the budget of a woman, like Mary Timney, who lived in poverty. It is shown here to provide an illustration of a plaid or tartan dress of the period.

Appendix

Notes

One
1 – *The Kirkcudbright Advertister,* 24th January 1862
2 - *The Wigtownshire Free Press,* 23rd January 1862

Two
1 – *The Law and the Lady,* Wilkie Collins , Chatto and Windus, 1875
2 – *A Raking Pot of Tea, Consumption and Excess in Early Nineteenth Century Ireland,* Dr Helen O'Connell, Literature and History, 2012.

Three
1 – *National Records of Scotland, JC26/1862/101, Trial papers relating to Mary Timney for the crime of murder at Carsphad farm, Kells, Kirkcudbrightshire. Tried at High Court, Dumfries, 8 Apr 1862,* National Archives of Scotland, Edinburgh.
2 – *Statistical Account 1839* revised 1844. http stat-acc-scot.edina. ac.uk/link/1834–45/kirkcudbrightkells/.
3 – www.educationscotland.gov.uk
4 – *Great Day Out at the Gallows,* Neil Gow, www.heraldscotland.com
5 - *Building News and Architectural Review,* 1862, Google Books, stewartrysnippets.wordpress.com
6 – *Wigtownshire Free Press* BMD http://freepages.history.rootsweb. ancestry.com

Four
1 – *National Records of Scotland, JC26/1862/101, Trial papers relating to Mary Timney for the crime of murder at Carsphad farm, Kells, Kirkcudbrightshire. Tried at High Court, Dumfries, 8 Apr 1862,* National Archives of Scotland, Edinburgh.

2 – www.capitalpunishmentuk.org/scot1800.html

3 – Professor Clive Emsley, *Violent Crime, History Review 1998*, historytoday.com/clive-emsley/victorian-crime

4 – *Statistical Account 1839*, as before.

5 – *National Records of Scotland, JC26/1862/101, Trial papers relating to Mary Timney for the crime of murder at Carsphad farm, Kells, Kirkcudbrightshire. Tried at High Court, Dumfries, 8 Apr 1862*, National Archives of Scotland Edinburgh.

6 – The word referring to the beetle or mallet is almost indecipherable, the term batt is my interpretation of what is written in the document at Broughton House, Kirkcudbright.

Five,

1 – *National Records of Scotland, JC26/1862/101, Trial papers relating to Mary Timney for the crime of murder at Carsphad farm, Kells, Kirkcudbrightshire. Tried at High Court, Dumfries, 8 Apr 1862*, National Archives of Scotland

Six

1 – *Square Mile of Murder,* Jack House, The Molendinar Press, Glasgow 1975

2 – *Dictionary of National Biography,* London, Smith, Elder & Co. 1885–1900.

3 – The reporter of *The Kirkcudbright Advertiser* made several mistakes in notation of the jury which I have corrected with reference to the list of jurors in the indictment.

4 – There were several differences in the reporting of the case by the local newspapers, *The Dumfries Courier, The Dumfries Herald and Register, The Dumfries Standard and Advertiser, The Kirkcudbright Advertiser* and *The Wigtownshire Free Press.* I have used information from all of them to describe the trial.

5 – It is worth noting that the coverage of Dr Maclaggan's evidence

varied a great deal. One newspaper reported only the evidence that confirmed the accusation against Mary Timney and did not state that many of the items taken from her house by the police were not bloodstained or did not have bloodstains relating to the attack.

Seven

1 – Marie Manning was a Swiss born domestic servant who was hanged outside the Horsemonger Lane Gaol in England, on 13th of November 1849, after she and her husband were convicted of the murder of her lover, Patrick O'Connor, in the "Bermondsey Horror" case. It was the first time a husband and wife had been executed together in England since 1700.

Nine

1 – *The Hanging Tree, Execution and the English People 1777–1868*, V A C Gatrell, Oxford University Press, 1996.

2 – *The Hanging Tree*, as before.

3 – www.capitalpunishmentuk.org

4 – Calcraft had received death threats before the execution and after pulling the bolt he swiftly left the scaffold returning into the prison. The victim, swathed in bandages having attempted to kill himself the night before by throwing himself into a fire, managed to get his feet on the sides of the drop and drew himself back up only to be pushed off again by a member of the prison staff. When he, once again, managed to get his feet on the sides Calcraft was made to return to the scene and, before a now furious mob, hang on Bousfield's legs until he was strangled. This information comes from *The Hanging Tree*, details as before. As with the coverage of the trial, the quotes given for the execution come from a number of different local newspapers, unless specified, as listed before.

5 – *The Hanging Tree*, as before.

6 – A close-fitting linen cap formerly worn by women and children in Scotland.

Ten

1 – www.blackcountrymuse.com. This website gives an account of the case referred to by *The Walsall Free Press* when three young men robbed a pawnbrokers shop, the owner being killed during the robbery. Two were reprieved from being executed despite many people campaigning that they should all have received the same sentence.

2 – This was possibly the Castle Douglas writer Richard Hewat who was appointed to Mary's case. There is a statement contained in the archive of Broughton House which was made to him by Susan Timney in which she states that she did not see her mother take the 'batt' to Carsphad farmhouse though her statements to the police investigation appear to say the contrary.

Eleven

1 – It is worth mentioning here that there had been a tradition of holding executions not only in the nearest town but also at the exact spot where the crime was committed but this had not been the case for many years by 1862.

2 – www.publications.parliament.uk

3 – www.stephen-stratford.co.uk

4 – *Certain Other Countries, Homicide, Gender and National Identity in Late 19th Century England, Ireland, Scotland and Wales,* Carolyn A Conley, Ohio State Press, 2007.

5 – As before.

Twelve

1 – *The Hanging Tree Execution and the English People 1777–1868*, V A C Gatrell
2 – *William Ewart: Portrait of a Radical*, W A Munford.Grafton and Co, 1960.
3 – As before.
4 – As before
5 – *The Hanging Tree* as before

Thirteen

1 – *Southern Counties Asylum case book 9th December 1858 to 22nd January 1862*. Other cases at the time had causes such as 'use of intoxicating liquors' 'ill usage' 'fatigue' 'small pox' and 'supposed to be melancholy.'
2 – Traditionally harvest is August/September time with Harvest Festivals usually held at the end of September.

Fourteen

1 – The statement by Frank Timney is not with the precognition papers in Edinburgh. A copy of it is in the archive at Broughton House in Kirkcudbright.
2 – As before the word is actually virtually indecipherable, batt is my interpretation. The context of the sentence makes it clear she means the implement later referred to as the beetle or mallet.

Fifteen

1 – *Women Who Kill*, Ann Jones, Victor Gollancz, 1991.
2 – *The Carsphad Tragedy 13th January 1862: A Memorial Poem*, Alexander Wilson published by his grandson Keith D Wilson in January 2007.
3 – http://archiver.rootsweb.ancestry.com/th/read/SCT-WIGTOWNSHIRE/2010-03/1267722352 and http://gdl.cdlr.strath.ac.uk/haynin/haynin1604.htm

Sources

www.blackcountrymuse.com
wikipedia.org
planetslade.com/broadside-ballads-jealous-annie
educationscotland.gov.uk
old-kirkcubright.net
britishnewspaperarchive.co.uk
kirkcudbright.co.uk
stewartrysnippets.wordpress.com
churchofscotland.org.uk
stephen-stratford.co.uk
capitalpunishmentuk.org/scot
edinphoto.org.uk
scottish-places.info/scotgaz/towns/townhistory349.html
bbc.co.uk/history/british/victorians/crime
heraldscotland.com
familysearch.org
scotlandspeople.co.uk
genesreunited.co.uk
historytoday.com/clive-emsley/victorian-crime
stat-acc-scot.edina.ac.uk
readdurhamenglish.wordpress.com
freepages.history.rootsweb.ancestry.com
http://gdl.cdlr.strath.ac.uk/haynin/haynin1604.htm
http://archiver.rootsweb.ancestry.com/th/read/
    SCTWIGTOWNSHIRE/2010-03/1267722352
maps.nls.uk
surnamedb.com
churchofscotland.org.uk
theglenkens.org.uk
publications.parliament.uk
neal.oxborrow.net
www.dumgal.gov.uk/

All the local newspapers quoted in the book were read on microfiche at either Newton Stewart library or the Ewart library in Dumfries.

Bibliography

Conley, Carolyn, *Certain Other Countries, Homicide, Gender and National Identity in Late 19th Century Ireland, Scotland and Wales,* Ohio State University Press, 2007

Devine, T M, *Farm Servants and Labour in Lowland Scotland 1770 – 1914,* John Donald Publishers Ltd, Edinburgh, 1984.

Dick, The Rev. C H, *Highways and Byways in Galloway and Carrick,* G C Books, Wigtown, memorial edition 2001.

Duff, Charles, *A New Handbook on Hanging,* Panther, 1956

Dumfries and Galloway Family History Society Newsletter No. 66 November 2009

Flanders, Judith, *The Invention of Murder,* HarperPress. 2011.

Gatrell, V A C, *The Hanging Tree, Execution and the English People 1770–1868.* Oxford University Press, 1996.

House, Jack, *Square Mile of Murder,* The Molendinar Press, Glasgow 1975

Jones, Ann, *Women Who Kill,* Victor Gollancz 1991

Macdonald, John H A, *A Practical Treatise on the Criminal Law of Scotland,* William Paterson, Edinburgh, 1867.

O'Connell, Helen, *A Raking Pot of Tea, Consumption and Excess in Early Nineteenth Century Ireland,* Literature and History 2012.

Paterson, Michael, *Life in Victorian Britain, A Social History of Queen Victoria's Reign,* Robinson, 2008.

Pow, Tom, *The Execution of Mary Timney,* Radio Play broadcast by BBC Radio Scotland in 1990.

Wiener, Martin J, *Men of Blood, Violence, Manliness and Criminal Justice in Victorian England,* Cambridge University Press 2006

Wilson, Alexander, *Carsphad Tragedy, 13th January 1862 A Memorial Poem,* Keith D Wilson, Dumfries 2007.

Acknowledgements

Very great thanks go to Julia MacDonald of Clayhole Publishing who first told me about Mary Timney. My gratitude for their time and generosity also goes to Anna Campbell, Carphairn Heritage Group, Tom Pow, Donald Cowall, Professor Lindsay Farmer of the University of Glasgow, Graham Roberts, Alison Burgess and the staff at the Dumfries and Galloway Council Archives and Library Service, Joanne Turner, curator at Dumfries Museum, photographer Robin Baxter, book designer Mike Clayton, Dumfries and Galloway Family History Society, Sarah Jackson and the staff at the National Trust for Scotland property, Broughton House, Kirkcudbright. Special thanks also to Rob, Ruaridh, Connel and Floraidh Soutar who have to put up with my obsessions.

Illustration Credits

Writer and journalist Jayne Baldwin lives in Galloway along with her husband and three children. She is a director of the children's publishing company Curly Tale Books Ltd and the author of 'West Over the Waves, The Final Flight of Elsie Mackay' and 'The Belties of Curleywee Farm.'